Hermit Cra

Hermit Crabs as

Hermit Crabs book for care,

interaction, diet and costs.

By

Louis Bridge

Published by: Zoodoo Publishing

Table of Contents

Introduction

In this book, we are going to look at the Hermit Crab (*Dardanus calidus*). The Hermit Crab is an oceanic animal. A marine crustacean, which can be found either in the ocean or on beaches. The Hermit Crab is a crustacean known as a *Decapoda crustacean*. Sometimes they are known as decapods for short.

These Decapoda crustaceans involve a large family of other marine animals. These other marine animals include crabs, lobsters, shrimps, prawns and crayfish. There are literally thousands of this species and most of them are scavengers.

In other words, Decapoda crustaceans will eat whatever they can get hold of. They will eat dead plants or dead animals. Decapoda crustaceans are both carnivorous and herbivorous, meaning that they will eat both meat and plant based foods.

The Hermit Crab is found all over the world. You can find Hermit Crabs in oceans all over the world. Depending on where they are found in the world, their look slightly alters. Their look slightly alters because they have different colours. Hermit Crabs have different colours, depending on where you find them. They can come in a wide variety of colours, from red to brown.

To start off this book, we are going to look at 'What is a Hermit Crab?' That is our first chapter. We will be explaining and analysing what exactly a Hermit Crab is. We have already explained that Hermit Crabs are a crustacean, but, we will be going into a deeper analysis of what a Hermit Crab is in Chapter 1.

There is a lot of information that you will learn about the species known as Hermit Crabs in chapter 1. This first chapter is set to be an introduction to the marine animal Hermit Crabs. We shall start off the chapter describing what exactly a Hermit Crab is.

They are exactly what you would expect them to be; the Hermit Crab is a species of crab which belong to the crab family. However, the Hermit Crab is much more than this. The Hermit Crab is much larger than just any other crab - they are a fantastic species with a lot of personality.

When you starting reading about the Hermit Crab and learning about the Hermit Crab, you are going to see just how wonderful this little marine animal is. They will capture your imagination and your heart.

We will then go onto show you where in the world you can find Hermit Crabs. By the name 'crab', you are probably aware that you will find this species in the ocean, or near the ocean. That is one of the habitats they inhabit, but, they are found in so many more habitats than that.

Their habitats will depend upon whether they are marine Hermit Crabs or land Hermit Crabs. That is the two distinct types of Hermit Crabs; marine Hermit Crabs and land Hermit Crabs. Because the Hermit Crab can be found in such a wide variety of habitats, it makes them widespread across the world.

This is something that we will explore more in-depth in Chapter 1.

We will also be going in-depth a bit about many other things about Hermit Crabs. These things include the biology of Hermit Crabs, the anatomy of Hermit Crabs and the sea shells of Hermit Crabs. There is so much to explore about Hermit Crabs in this first chapter, which will pave the way for the rest of the book, and for chapter two.

In Chapter 2, we are going to look at the predators of Hermit Crabs. You might be wondering what the predators of Hermit Crabs are? Or more specifically, you might be wondering about what it means when we say the predators of Hermit Crabs? What we mean when we say the predators of Hermit Crabs, are marine or land animals that hunt and eat Hermit Crabs.

We will not only be looking at what marine animals and what land animals eat Hermit Crabs, we will also be looking at what Hermit Crabs eat. You may be wondering what these adorable sea creatures eat. Do they eat other animals? Do they eat plant-based food? What do Hermit Crabs eat?

The truth is, Hermit Crabs eat both, they eat both other animals and plant based foods. Hermit Crabs are opportunists when it comes to food, this is something we will examine more in Chapter 3.

Chapter 3 will focus on what Hermit Crabs eat. In this chapter we are going to look at what Hermit Crabs eat both in the wild and while as a pet. Their diet can vary a little from being a pet to being in the wild.

The thing about Hermit Crabs is that they are not eaters which are choosy about what they eat. Hermit Crabs will literally eat almost anything they come across.

They won't try and kill anything they come across, but, if they see a dead animal lying around then they will eat it if they are hungry enough.

You will find out in this book about what Hermit Crabs eat while on land and what they eat while in the sea. Being exposed to a wide variety of foods can help this little animal survive quite well in the wild.

As a pet, you will find out what to feed your Hermit Crab. You are going to be feeding your Hermit Crab both specialized food and food such as vegetables. Chapter Three is a very important chapter, as feeding your Hermit Crab the right foods is very important to their survival.

At the beginning of Chapter 4, we will take the book in the next direction. We will be looking at how you can get started on your journey to having a pet Hermit Crab.

We start off the next section of the book in chapter four with a how-to, step-by-step guide of how you can get a pet Hermit Crab. The step-by-step guide is there to make it easy for you to get started with your new pet.

It is also aimed to help simply the steps you need to take in having a Hermit Crab as a pet and caring for a Hermit Crab as a pet. Don't be daunted by the list of things that you need to do to look after and care for your Hermit Crab. All pets need the same amount of care and attention.

It's just easier to get started with animals such as cats and dogs as pets, because we are very familiar with them as pets. However, because not many people have Hermit Crabs as pets, you are probably not as familiar with them.

As you are not as familiar with them, you probably don't know much about Hermit Crabs, or how to look after them. Therefore, we have provided you with a great step-by-step guide on how to look after your pet crab.

You will learn many things about the Hermit Crab. Including things such as what you will need for your new pet Hermit Crab. And what you will need to feed him. The step-by-step guide provides more information than that though.

It also provides you with information such as: what to put in your tank and what temperature your tank should be for your Hermit Crab.

A good idea for you would be to print out the step-by-step guide. That way you will be able to follow the guide easily, without having to go through this entire book again. Though, it is a good idea to refresh yourself with this book, read it a few times to get familiar with the Hermit Crab.

As we progress towards Chapter 5, we will be looking at the essential equipment that you will need for your new pet Hermit Crab. Like with any pet, there are certain things that you will need to buy for your new pet. Preferably you should buy your equipment before you buy your new pet Hermit Crab.

In Chapter 5, we will be looking at the equipment that you will need to buy. We will be looking at things you need to buy for your pet, such as foods and accommodation. The accommodation that you will buy for your pet (the pet Hermits new crab); will be part of your consideration of how to home your new pet.

There are a few things that you will need to buy for your Hermit Crab. These things are the essential items that you need to buy for your pet Hermit Crab. Things such as sand, a tank, food water and some toys.

There may be a lot that you need to buy for your new Hermit Crab. However, it isn't really that much more than say a pet hamster or a pet rabbit. Plus, buying your equipment for Hermit Crabs is very easy.

You can find most of the stuff for Hermit Crabs on line. In the book we have given you an excellent selection of websites that you can go to in order to purchase your Hermit Crab equipment.

In Chapter 6, we will be looking at another thing you should consider when you are homing your new pet crab. And that is the environment of your home. By this, we partly mean things such as the temperature of your home. Having the temperature of your home at a comfortable level for your pet crab.

The temperature of your home is only one aspect of your home environment that you should consider. There are two other things that you should consider when purchasing a Hermit Crab (1) The people who are in your household, and (2) Other pets that you may have in the house.

As we move onto Chapter 7, we are going to look at how you can and should hold your pet Hermit Crab. And also, how you can make sure that your new Hermit Crab gets the exercise he needs.

You will learn why the Hermit Crab is sensitive, through learning about the Hermit Crabs anatomy and biology. Learning about their anatomy and biology shows you how sensitive they are.

As crabs are gentle and sensitive animals, it is important to learn how to hold them properly and how to give them enough exercise, so that they remain fit and healthy. There are many forms of exercise that your Hermit Crab can take, which is listed in this book.

The exercise that Hermit Crabs can take are things such as walking about, being took out of their tank and into a bigger sand pit, or having toys and a hamster wheel.

Try and have as many of these as you can for your Hermit Crab. Not only will it give your Hermit Crab some exercise, it will also give them something fun to do.

You will also learn in this chapter how to hold your Hermit Crab. Knowing how to how your Hermit Crab is very important. You don't want to hold your Hermit Crab too tight. And neither do you want to hold your Hermit Crab too loosely. Somewhere in between is perfect.

Chapter 8 will focus on the nocturnal nature of Hermit Crabs. If you are unfamiliar with Hermit Crabs, then, you will be unfamiliar with their natural and behaviour. This includes their nocturnal behaviour.

If you are not familiar with Hermit Crabs, then you should know that these species are nocturnal in nature. To be nocturnal in nature means to be active at night. Therefore, you should really take this into consideration before buying a Hermit Crab.

With Hermit Crabs being nocturnal, it means that you will have to do everything for them at night. This includes things such as you having to feed and water them at night, having to play with them at night and having to clean out their tank at night. Make sure that you are up for this, prepared for this and can do this for your Hermit Crab.

These are things that you should be taking into consideration before you buy your Hermit Crab. Not afterwards.

In the last chapter of this book about Hermit Crabs, chapter nine, chapter nine will focus on how you can get the best out of your Hermit Crab.

There are many ways to get the best out of your Hermit Crab, which we will explore in this book. One of the best ways to get the best out of your Hermit Crab is to look after him, make sure that he is healthy and happy, and make sure that he eats and drinks the right things.

Another great way to get the best out of your Hermit Crab is to bond with him and make the most out of him. Spend time with him and enjoy him. We hope that this book will help to teach you how to bond with your Hermit Crab.

If you do learn how to bond with your Hermit Crab well, then you will have a rewarding time with your pet Hermit Crab.

The main way to bond well through your Hermit Crab is by loving him and treating him right. Thank you for purchasing this book. We hope that you enjoy it!

Chapter 1. What is a Hermit Crab?

You may be wondering, 'What is a Hermit Crab?' In this chapter, we are going to explain to you what are Hermit Crab is. So, 'What is a Hermit Crab?' Let us take a look at what a Hermit Crab is.

Hermit Crabs are a fascinating marine animal. They come in a wide variety of colours, from a deep red colour to a pinkish salmon colour and even a brown colour. Hermit Crabs rely on shells to protect them from harm, as they have a soft abdomen and can easily become vulnerable to predators. You can find Hermit Crabs in a variety of places. Mostly Hermit Crabs are found in the ocean. However, they can be found washed up on the beach. Depending on where the Hermit Crabs are found, will determine what colour they are.

The Species of Hermit Crabs

There are over 1000 different species of Hermit Crabs in the wild. Most of those different species of Hermit Crab have a soft abdomen. This is particularly important to remember when you hold your pet crab. We will go into this in a lot more detail later in the book. The abdomen of most hermit crabs is not only soft.

The Biology Of Hermit Crabs

Most hermit crabs also share other biological features. The other features that most hermit crabs tend to have are that most hermit crabs are long and most hermit crabs have curved abdomens. This makes them quite different from other crustaceans. Other crustaceans have hard shells and bodies. The soft makeup of the Hermit Crab can make them particularly vulnerable to predators. Whether those predators are on land or at sea. The Hermit Crab has a shell to protect them from predators in the wild. The seashell of the Hermit Crab protects their vulnerable abdomen. The Hermit Crab can retract into this seashell, protecting their whole body.

The Sea Shells Of Hermit Crabs

The Hermit Crab will take seashells from other species. Mostly Hermit Crabs will steal seashells from sea snails.

In the wild Hermit Crabs will take up almost any sea shell that they find, if it is big enough for them to hide under. This offers them great protection.

Where Can I Find Hermit Crabs?

The danger posed to Hermit Crabs from other species in the wild, will depend upon where in the World you find the Hermit Crab.

Species of Hermit Crabs are found in areas on the beach such as rock pools. The rock pool is the Hermit Crabs favourite place to be.

For those of you who are unfamiliar with the term rock pool, let us just explain what a rock pool is to you. A rock pool is usually found on a beach, mostly close to the sea. They are basically small ponds, with rocks around them.

Hence their name, the rock pool is really a small pool with rocks around and in it. What is interesting is what is in these pools themselves. Rock pools are home to, or receive visitors, of several marine species. One of these species is the Hermit Crab.

The Habitat Of The Hermit Crab

The rock pool is one of the habitats of the Hermit Crab in the wild, but, it is not the only habitat of the Hermit Crab.

The Hermit Crab can be found in a number of different habitats. You will find Hermit Crabs in the following habitats: the deep sea ocean, the sea bed, the intertidal zone and estuaries.

You will find Hermit Crabs in the following places: Australia, Europe, the Americas and Africa.

Commonly Used Names For The Hermit Crab

Hermit Crabs are and can be identified by their names.
The Hermit Crabs common and most well-known is simply 'The Hermit Crab.' However, there are other names which are given to the Hermit Crab. The Hermit Crabs Latin name is *Paguroidea*. Their class name is the *Malacostraca*. And their order name is the *Decapoda*. Hermit Crabs will also have their own lasting names depending on what species of Hermit Crab there is.

There are around 1000 species of Hermit Crab worldwide. Each of these 1000 species of Hermit Crab, has their own unique Latin names.

Latin names are given to animals, including marine animals such as the Hermit Crab, in order to help identify them. Each Latin name is different and unique, which makes the species of Hermit Crab more easy to identify.

Using a name that is easily identifiable can help us with conserving Hermit Crabs in the wild, and it serves the purpose of exploring and learning about the anatomy of the Hermit Crab.

The Anatomy Of Hermit Crabs

The anatomy of any animal is important. Studying and learning about an animal's anatomy can help us better understand them. It can also help us to conserve Hermit Crabs in the wild if they are endangered. And it can help us to find cures for diseases or illnesses that the animal may have; which in turn help us to either prevent those diseases and illnesses, or cure those diseases and illnesses in Hermit Crabs.

There is a lot going on with the anatomy of the Hermit Crab. As Hermit Crabs are animals which are both marine animals and land animals, their anatomy can be quite different than species of animals which are only marine animals or only land animals.

As the Hermit Crab is not specifically a marine animal or a land animal (it is both), their anatomy can be quite different and complex compared with other species of animals. The complexity of this species anatomy makes their anatomy fascinating to observe.

The Skin Of The Hermit Crab

A noticeable part of the Hermit Crabs anatomy is their skin. Particularly their exoskeleton skin. The exoskeleton skin is particularly noticeable because it is the area of skin which the Hermit Crab shed. The Hermit Crab sheds their exoskeleton skin so that they can grow a new, stronger layer of skin.

The exoskeleton skin is the hard, outer layer of the crab's skin. This area of the skin is essential for the Hermit Crab, as it acts as a layer of protection for them. Protection from things such as predators or being hurt by harmful objects to the crab. The exoskeleton area of the skin is also made up of other things which form the Hermit Crabs skin anatomy. These things include the *carapace*, which is the hard shield in the exoskeleton skin, and the *setae*, which are the sensory hairs found in the exoskeleton skin.

The Senses Of The Hermit Crab

The Hermit Crab has various senses of which they are composed. The compound eyes of the Hermit Crab are comprised of facet lenses. These eyes are moveable, which help protect them from predators.

Their feelers are another sensory area of the Hermit Crab. The feelers are also called the Antennae. The *Antennae* area of the Hermit Crab is comprised of sensory organs, which helps gives the crab information about their surroundings.

The *Antennae* helps give the crab information about their surroundings because the crabs can use this area of their body to touch things and feel things which are in the crab's path. It helps the crab to navigate through its surroundings and helps them to avoid anything which may be in the crab path.

Another area of the Hermit Crabs anatomy which helps them to get a feel of something is their mouth. This area is known as the *Millipedes*. The mouth of the Hermit Crab has senses, senses which send signals to the crab's brain about whether or not the crab's taste buds like something or dislike something.

The mouth area of the Hermit Crab works in three ways. First, it works to taste food. Second, it works to help the crab groom itself. And thirdly, it helps to pick up food and eat it.

Hermit Crabs can also pick up their food with their claws. They pinch the food and insert the food into their mouths. These claws are known as Chelipeds. The Chelipeds are used to grab things and pinch things. It can also be used for defence. The Hermit Crab will defend itself using this area of their body.

There are two claws on the front of the Hermit Crab, they have a long claw and leg, and a smaller claw and leg. Both perform different functions.

The smaller Hermit Crab is used for the crab feeding himself and helping himself drink water. While the larger claw is used to pinch and attack, basically the larger claw is used by the Hermit Crab to defend itself.

The Legs Of The Hermit Crab

The leg area of the Hermit Crab is called the *Pereiopods*. The Hermit Crabs legs can be very vulnerable. Often, they are so vulnerable that they can fall off. That is how sensitive they are.

That's why you shouldn't put anything in the Hermit Crabs tank which will harm them. Their legs can be damaged very easily, which is why it is best to make sure that nothing can harm them in their tank.

If you put things like balls into your crabbit, make sure that they don't have holes or gaps in them, as the crab's legs can get caught in them and break easily.

The legs of the Hermit Crabs have different functions. One of the functions of the Hermit Crabs legs is to groom and clean. Another function of their legs is to walk and move about.

How The Hermit Crabs Breathes: Their Gills

Finally, and probably the most important area of the Hermit Crabs anatomy is their gills. The gills are the area of the Hermit Crab with which they breathe. Without their gills, they would suffocate and die. They are the area and the organ with which the crab breathes.

This is where it becomes important in looking after the Hermit Crab. It is important to look after the Hermit Crab by making sure that the air is moist enough for the Hermit Crab.

The Species Of Hermit Crabs

There are many different Species Of Hermit Crabs; there are 1000 different species of Hermit Crabs. These 1000 species of Hermit Crabs are a diverse bunch of animals. They are diverse in their habitats in which they live, their colour, size, shape, behaviour and personality.

The Hermit Crab is determined by its anatomy. It is in their anatomy that most Hermit Crabs are different animals, though the difference is slight, which is why they belong to the same family.

Most Hermit Crabs have a similar anatomy, even though there are hundreds of different species of Hermit Crabs.

Given that there are hundreds of different species of Hermit Crabs, they are a diverse group, which have different colours, sizes and shapes.

Although we aren't going to go into all of the 1000 different species of Hermit Crabs in-depth. We are going to take a look at the physicality of Hermit Crabs; their colours, their sizes and their shapes.

The Look Of The Hermit Crab

All of the Hermit Crab species have their own different look. In other words, all Hermit Crabs have their own appearance. Because all Hermit Crabs have their own appearance, it can make them easily recognisable and distinguishable from other Hermit Crabs.

Let us take the colour of your Hermit Crab first. The colour of your Hermit Crab is going to be determined by the species of Hermit Crab he is. Hermit Crabs come in a variety of colours. The most common colours for Hermit

Crabs are orange, brown, yellow and red. Although Hermit Crabs can appear in several colours.

The colour of the Hermit Crab can also be determined by his age. As the Hermit Crab sheds his skin, he can take on a different colour, as he matures. As Hermit Crabs mature, they can and will look different from when they were young and when you first had them. While he is shedding his skin, the Hermit Crab can take on a pinkish colour. This doesn't last though, when he has grown his new skin, he will have a different colour of skin.

Hermit Crabs don't just come in different colours; they also come in different sizes and shapes. Hermit Crabs are small compared with most other animals. However, they vary in size. The biggest that the Hermit Crab can grow is up to about the size of an adult palm. Due to their small size, the Hermit Crab is vulnerable to many predators in the wild.

This is why Hermit Crabs take shell. The shells are used to protect them from predators. The average size of a Hermit Crab is 2-10cm. They do not get much bigger than 10cm.Although Hermit Crabs are quite different in size, they are not that much different in shape. They have a similar shape to other crabs. With shells that take on the shape of coconuts.

The Species Of Hermit Crabs Available As Pets

You won't find all 1000 species of Hermit Crab available as pets, but two main ones are the Caribbean Hermit Crab and the Ecuadorian Hermit Crab. These two species of Hermit Crab are exotic species and they are the two species which are most commonly sold in pet stores.

The Caribbean Hermit Crab (Coenobita clypeus), is probably the most common species of Hermit Crab. They come in a pinkish/red colour; though can often turn brownish as they mature. And, will often take on white sea shells. They are native to North America and South America.

The Caribbean Hermit Crab is a land Hermit Crab. They are known for their tree activity; where they climb trees in the wild. They will also get underneath trees, as they bury underneath the trees roots. This can make observing the species in the wild a wonderful natural phenomenon.

The Ecuadorian Hermit Crab looks quite different from the Caribbean Hermit Crab. It is not as colourful or attractive as the Caribbean Hermit Crab, though it is a cute pet in its own right. The Ecuadorian Hermit Crab is not as striking, they don't have the same striking colours as the Hermit Crab. The Ecuadorian Hermit Crab is smaller, as well as different in colour.

This species of crab is a brownish colour, with dashes of white running through it.

In the wild, they can be found in either the Pacific or in countries such as Chile or Equador, hence its name. Unlike the Caribbean Hermit Crab, the Ecuadorian Hermit Crab can be found in different habitats. They are more of a marine Hermit Crab, which can be found in places such as tidal pools.

Both of these different Hermit Crabs will require different care. Although they are both a species of Hermit Crab, they require a different approach to caring for them as pets, due to one being a land Hermit Crab and the other being a marine Hermit Crab.

Teaching Your Hermit Crab To Do Tricks

A fantastic reason to buy a pet Hermit Crab is that you can teach them to do tricks. In that sense, Hermit Crabs as pets are like dogs. It will keep both you and your Hermit Crab entertained. Many people teach their Hermit Crabs to do tricks, and so can you!

You are going to need a lot of time and patience to teach your Hermit Crab tricks. It will take your Hermit Crab a while to learn the tricks you teach him. And, therefore, it will take a lot of patience on your part to teach him these new tricks. However, if you do have the patience to teach your crab tricks, it can be a rewarding experience. If you want to teach your Hermit Crab tricks, here are some guidelines on how to do it.

- ***Teach him at night***

Teach your Hermit Crab these new tricks at night. Both because it is a nocturnal species and because their brains are more active at night. As their brains are more active at night, it helps them learn better. And therefore, you will teach your Hermit Crab to learn these new tricks at a quicker pace.

- ***Take Out Some Food***

When you are training your Hermit Crab to perform new tricks, you will want to have some food nearby. Like all animals, if you have some food to feed your Hermit Crab, then you can teach your Hermit Crab to perform new tricks quicker.

- ***Talk To Your Hermit Crab***

By talking to your Hermit Crab you can help bond with your Hermit Crab, let him bond with you and become familiar with you and you will let him know and learn how to do tricks.

- ***Types Of Tricks***

Some people train their Hermit Crabs to ring bells. A good way to teaching your Hermit Crab to ring a bell is to put a piece of their food on the bell. This will train them to ring the bell.

The Hermit Crab can be easy to train if you have the patience to train him. However, it takes a lot of patience, time and energy to train a crab. Have patience and you will be rewarded with a great pet who can do tricks.

Their ability to learn tricks is one of the reasons that these animals are intelligent. Hermit Crabs are intelligent animals. Hermit Crabs are known for their resilience, for outsmarting other animals who choose to hunt them and eat them. Hermit Crabs are also known to learn from their mistakes.

The ability of the Hermit Crab to learn from their mistakes shows a high intelligence in the animal. For example, Hermit Crabs will try and avoid things which got them into trouble, such as crossing a predator which almost killed them. They also avoid food which has made them ill before.

Hermit Crabs have an impressive intelligence for their size and species. We only think of animals such as apes as having intelligence. But, the Hermit Crabs prove this to be wrong.

How To Bathe Your Hermit Crab

Giving your Hermit Crab a bath is one of the key ways to look after your Hermit Crab. It is an essential way to look after your crab.

If you are new to Hermit Crabs and want to know how to bathe them, then, look no further, we are going to give you some easy steps to do so.

- ***Why You Should Give Your Hermit Crab A Bath***

There are many good reasons why you should give your Hermit Crab a bath. Here we are going to explore the important reasons of why you should give your Hermit Crab a bath.

Hermit Crabs, like other pets, need to have a bath. Or, they need to remain clean. Hermit Crabs as pets can't really wash themselves, so, it is up to you to wash your Hermit Crab for him, and therefore, make sure that he is kept clean.

That is one of the reasons that it is essential to bath a Hermit Crab, you need to bathe him to keep him clean. This is not the only reason that you should bathe your Hermit Crab. The other reason is, to ensure that he doesn't catch mites.

- ***Prepare The Bath For Your Crab***

Now that you know why you should bathe your Hermit Crab, you are now going to know how to prepare your bath.

You should prepare the bath before you take your Hermit Crab out of his tank. This ensures that you can fill up the bath and prepare the bath, without also looking after your Hermit Crab at the same time. You will also be keeping him free of danger. If he is left wandering about while you are preparing the bath, you may accidentally step on him.

- ***Filling The Bath For Your Hermit Crab***

You will need something to bathe the Hermit Crab in. A bowl or a container will be perfect for bathing your Hermit Crab in. You can buy this bowl or container when you are buying your other equipment for your Hermit Crab. And keep it separately from your other dishes. Put it away with your sand and food, keep all the stuff together, then the bowl will be easy to find when you want to bathe your Hermit Crab.

Make sure your bowl or container is not too deep, but, deep enough to bathe your Hermit Crab. Once you have your bowl or container, you will want to fill the bowl or container up with water. Never bathe your Hermit Crab in tap water. Tap water can be lethal to Hermit Crabs.

Instead, you will want to bathe your Hermit Crab in salt water. What you should do is add fresh water to the bowl or container. Then you should add Hermit Crab salt to the fresh water. Never put table salt into the bathing water. After you have done that, give it a good stir. Make sure that the salt is blended well in the water. You should add about a table spoon of salt to your water. Nothing else should be added to the water, only the Hermit Crab salt. Once you have done this, you are ready for the next step.

- ***Bathing Your Hermit Crab***

Once you have prepared your Hermit Crabs bath, though, not too high, make sure that the bath is not too deep for your Hermit Crab, your next step is to bath your Hermit Crab.

To bath your Hermit Crab, you want to start by introducing him to the water slowly. This is especially true if you are bathing him in the bath for the first time, as the water will be unfamiliar to him. You will want to take it easy.

Make sure that the water in your bath is not going to the Hermit Crabs shell, you don't want him to drown. To ensure he doesn't drown, you can also put in the bath a log and some rocks. That gives him something to climb on, which can avoid him from drowning.

Like humans, being in under water for too long can kill Hermit Crabs. They need oxygen to breathe. If they are submerged in water and cannot get out, then they will drown. A good way for you to avoid your Hermit Crab drowning is to place one of your palms below the Hermit Crab. That means you can catch him if he goes under water and it will give him a sense of security if he feels your palm.

Therefore, you should never leave your Hermit Crab unattended while in the bath. It wouldn't take very long for him to drown. You should and must make sure that you supervise your Hermit Crab at all times. You won't need to bathe him for long anyway.

- ***Watching Your Hermit Crab***

When you have put your Hermit Crab in the water, your next step is to wash your Hermit Crab. Washing your Hermit Crab is fairly easy because of the Hermit Crabs smooth skin and shell.

You can either wash your Hermit Crab with your hands or, you can wash your Hermit Crab with a soft sponge. Either method you choose to wash your Hermit Crab, do it gently. Slowly rub him with either your hand or a soft sponge while in the bath.

- ***How Often Should You Bathe A Hermit Crab?***

You should bathe your Hermit Crab every week, perhaps two weeks. Water and baths can stress the Hermit Crab out, which is one reason to avoid bathing them on a regular basis. Also, Hermit Crabs don't get as dirty as other pets do, such as dogs. When you have a dog, you need to bathe it more regularly, as they get dirty more easily.
With Hermit Crabs, this isn't true. It also doesn't take that long to bathe a Hermit Crab. You should bathe your Hermit Crab in little to no time.

That's it, six easy steps on how to prepare your Hermit Crabs bath and how to bathe your Hermit Crabs bath. Preparing your Hermit Crabs bath and bathing your Hermit Crab is an easy and straight forward experience.

Bonding With Your Hermit Crab

Bathing your Hermit Crab is one of the ways to bond with your Hermit Crab, but, there are other ways that you can bond with your Hermit Crab.

Bonding with your Hermit Crab is a great way to care for your Hermit Crab. It is also a great way to entertain your Hermit Crab and look after him.

Bonding with your Hermit Crab is the most rewarding aspect of having a Hermit Crab. You get to give your Hermit Crab love, affection and care, while, at the same time, your Hermit Crab gives you love and affection back. Pets are known to increase health and wellbeing in the owners of pets. The Hermit Crab is no different in increasing health and wellness in their owners.

Bonding with your Hermit Crab will require your time. To bond well with your Hermit Crab, you will have to give him plenty of your time. This ensures that he is also looked after well.

There are several ways that you can bond with your pet crab. Let us take a look at how you can bond with your pet crab.

- ***Spend Time With Him***

The first step to bonding with your Hermit Crab and the most important step in bonding with your Hermit Crab is to spend time with your Hermit Crab.

Spending time with your Hermit Crab has many important benefits. One of the benefits of bonding with your Hermit Crab is that it gives your Hermit Crab love and affection. Another benefit of your Hermit Crab is that it keeps your Hermit Crab healthy and in good shape.

- ***Help Him Exercise***

Helping your pet Hermit Crab to exercise, is another great way to bond with your Hermit Crab.

It is a great way to bond with your Hermit Crab because it lets your Hermit Crab have fun while giving your Hermit Crab fun at the same time. You will have great times by bonding with your Hermit Crab in this way.

- ***Learning About Your Hermit Crab***

Learning about your Hermit Crab is the third and final way to bond with your Hermit Crab. Learning about your Hermit Crab helps you learn about what and who a Hermit Crab is. This can and will increase the bonding between you and your Hermit Crab because you will know more about your Hermit Crab.

Bonding with your Hermit Crab is a very fun experience. One which you will enjoy and your Hermit Crab will enjoy. Make the most of it!

Breeding Your Hermit Crab

Breeding your Hermit Crab is something that some pet owners of the Hermit Crab will want to do. With other people, it is not a step that they will want to take. For those of you who do want to breed your Hermit Crab, there is a straight forward way that you can breed it.

Breeding Hermit Crabs is not for the faint hearted - it can be a challenging experience. Though, if you want to breed them it can be both rewarding and a way for you to have more Hermit Crabs without buying them.

If you want to breed your Hermit Crab, you will have to have two Hermit Crabs. Make sure that the crabs get on well. One of these Hermit Crabs should be male, the other Hermit Crab should be female.

Once you have done this, create a suitable environment for them to breed. An environment which is relaxing, warm and comforting.

The Downsides Of Having A Pet Hermit Crab

Although having a pet Hermit Crab is a great experience, there are also some downsides to having a Hermit Crab as a pet.

One of the main downsides to having a Hermit Crab as a pet is that they are an exotic species. In being an exotic species, this can make it hard to find the things you need for Hermit Crabs, such as food, water and their essential equipment.

This is because this stuff is not in high demand, as the Hermit Crab is not a popular pet. Therefore, their essential items are not wanted by many people. This can make buying stuff for the Hermit Crab challenging. Another downside to the Hermit Crab is their nocturnal nature. Their nocturnal nature means that you won't see them out much during daylight hours.

It means that you may only see them out during the night, or during the early morning hours. This can be disappointing; at it gives you less time to bond with your Hermit Crab.

Finally, the last downside to having a pet Hermit Crab is their lifespan. In the wild, Hermit Crabs can live for up to 20 years. The sad thing is, as a pet, they usually only live for around a year. Which means you won't have them for that long.

Otherwise, there isn't anything else that is disappointing about the Hermit Crab or having the Hermit Crab as a pet. Their positive attributes that they bring to your life, far outweigh any negatives. That is why they are such a great pet to have!

Common Illnesses And Diseases In Hermit Crab

There are various common illnesses and diseases in Hermit Crabs. Let us take a look at what the common illnesses and diseases of the Hermit Crabs are. They are listed in no particular order. And should be cured by taking him to a vet the minute you spot your Hermit Crab having any of these illnesses or diseases.

- ***Mites***

Mites are one of the most common things to happen to Hermit Crabs in captivity and as pets.

Hermit Crabs will get mites if they are not looked after properly, or if their tanks are not cleaned out regularly enough.

That is why it is so important to both bathe your Hermit Crab and clean his tank out, both on a regular basis. If you bathe your Hermit Crab regularly and clean your tank out regularly, then you will prevent your Hermit Crab from catching mites.

- ***The Hermit Crab's Skin Rotting***

Another sign that your Hermit Crab is not well and has an illness or a disease, is when his skin is rotting. If you find your Hermit Crabs skin rotting, then you should take him to the vet, don't leave it for too long. If a vet can treat it early, then he has a good chance of overcoming it and getting back to full health.

Rotting skin usually occurs in marine Hermit Crabs, and not so much in land Hermit Crabs. The reason for this is due to their different climate and biology.

The skin rotting attacks the exoskeleton skin, which means that your Hermit Crab can be particularly vulnerable to their skin rotting when the Hermit Crab is shedding its skin.
A good cure for rotting skin for Hermit Crabs is in giving them a bath. You can bathe your Hermit Crab gently in water and with a sponge. This will

help the rotting skin come off and prevent the disease from spreading. Never give your Hermit Crab any medicine which is not given to you by a vet.

Medication in animals should only be given on the advice of a vet. It is unlikely that any vet would give you medication for your pet Hermit Crab, as they don't work for Hermit Crabs. Only something like a little bath can Help a Hermit Crab overcome his illness or disease - which can be given from your home.

Daily Care For Hermit Crabs

There are daily care routines that you will have to perform for your pet Hermit Crab. This is true for all pets. No matter what pet you have, you have to carry out daily routines for that pet. Pets need your care and attention on a daily basis. Let us look at the daily care routines that you will have to perform for your pet Hermit Crab.

- ***Feeding Your Hermit Crab***

This is an obvious daily care routine that you will have to do for your Hermit Crab. Feeding your Hermit Crab is a daily activity. Make sure that your Hermit Crab has access to food on a daily basis. Often, at night time, Hermit Crabs can and will knock over their food. Sometimes Hermit Crabs will intentionally knock over their food.

Therefore, not only will you have to clean up the food that your Hermit Crab has knocked over and put it in the bin. You will also have to put some new fresh food into your Hermit Crabs bowl.

- ***Putting Fresh Water Out***

Just as having access to fresh food on a daily basis is essential for your Hermit Crab, so is having access to fresh water on a daily basis essential for your Hermit Crab. Your Hermit Crab will need new water daily. They will need both types of water on a daily basis, both fresh water and salt water. Therefore, this becomes one of the most essential elements of care that you will need to perform for your Hermit Crab.

Both of these types of water, both the fresh water and the salt water, are very essential for the Hermit Crab. These two types of water should never be mixed together. Instead, have one bowl with which you put the Hermit Crabs fresh water in. And have another bowl with which you put the Hermit Crabs salt water in.

- ***Check The Temperature On A Daily Basis***

The temperature of your home environment and the Hermit Crab's tank environment is very important to the Hermit Crab. If it is too hot, then the Hermit Crab will die, but they will die a slow and painful death. The same is true if the temperature is too cold for Hermit Crabs.

Therefore, it is very important to have the right temperature for Hermit Crabs. Much more than any other pet you may have, as the Hermit Crab is very sensitive and it does not adapt to change in temperature very well.

Humidity is very important for the Hermit Crab. Make sure that your home environment and the environment of your Hermit Crab's tank is kept at a humid temperature at all times.

- ***Grooming Your Pet Hermit Crab***

Grooming your pet Hermit Crab is another important daily activity. Grooming your pet Hermit Crab keeps him fresh and clean. This prevents diseases and illnesses taking hold of the Hermit Crab in the long run.

This can particularly stop things from mites taking over your Hermit Crab and taking over your Hermit Crab's tank. As they say, prevention is better than cure. And that is certainly the case with Hermit Crabs.

Chapter 2. Predators of Hermit Crabs

Hermit Crabs have many natural predators in the wild. They have many natural predators both on land and at sea. This is because the Hermit Crab is both a land animal, and a sea animal.

Due to the Hermit Crab being both a land animal and a sea animal, it means that they face twice the danger from predators.

For example, most animals are either a land animal, or a sea animal. Most animals are not both - in other words, most animals are not both sea animals as well as land animals. As such, they are exposed to fewer environments and less habitats. Because they are exposed to fewer environments and less habitats, they don't face as many dangers from predators.

When you are an animal such as the Hermit Crab, who is both exposed to land habitats and water habitats, then they face many more dangers than most other animals in the wild. What makes this worse for the Hermit Crab in the wild is that their bodies are vulnerable.

The bodies of Hermit Crabs are very sensitive and can easily break. This makes it easy for other animals to hunt and kill the Hermit Crab. And is probably one of the main reasons why the Hermit Crab faces so many dangers from predators in the wild.

Depending where you find the Hermit Crab, in other words, depending on where in the wild they are, what their habitats are in, will depend upon which predators pose danger to them.

Hermit Crabs who find their way onshore are vulnerable to predators such as birds. If birds find Hermit Crabs washed up on a beach, they will eat them if they are hungry. The Hermit Crab having a shell, or stealing a discarded shell from another marine animal, helps protect them.

They don't have to worry about birds when they are in the ocean much, as Hermit Crabs usually stay at the bottom of the ocean. Unless they are being washed onshore, then they are exposed to birds.

However, Hermit Crabs still face many natural predators while on the ocean sea bed. The Hermit Crab has many different natural predators in the ocean. And therefore, they have different threats in the ocean. Oceanic animals such as sharks, fish and squid, will and do eat Hermit Crabs. As they are quite small, they are vulnerable to being attacked and eaten by any predator which is bigger than the Hermit Crab.

In the sea, Hermit Crabs will bury underneath the sand to keep themselves out of the way of predators. In doing so, Hermit Crabs keep out of harm's way and are more likely to survive.

While on land, Hermit Crabs do hide under the sand and hide from dangers. However, they can be more vulnerable on land, because of the air element. It's more difficult for Hermit Crabs to see a predator from the air, than one which is swimming towards them.

This can give birds an advantage over Hermit Crabs. On land, Hermit Crabs are more vulnerable to being hunted and killed. They are more vulnerable because they can be killed by both humans and other animals.

The fact that Hermit Crabs live on the land and on the sea, means that they are particularly vulnerable. It makes these marine animals more vulnerable than most animals. This is particularly true because Hermit Crabs need to get a shell to help protect them.

Hermit Crabs need to steal other sea shells to help protect them from harm. The sea shells that they steal are bigger than the Hermit Crab itself. This allows the Hermit Crab to hide within the shell when either it feels threatened, or he faces imminent danger from a predator.

If the Hermit Crab was without a shell, then it would make them even more vulnerable to many predators., as they have a soft body and cannot protect themselves. This is especially true when they are young.

The soft body of the Hermit Crab makes it easy for predators to eat and digest. With a shell, it makes it difficult for predators to eat the Hermit Crab. The hard exterior of the Hermit Crab's shell helps to protect it.

When Hermit Crabs are young, they are more exposed to predators. Partly this is due to them not having a shell. And partly this has to do with them being young and inexperienced.

When they are inexperienced, they are vulnerable because they haven't learned how to protect themselves from predators.

Hiding inside their shells is one of the Hermit Crabs natural behaviours in the wild.

Hermit Crabs In The Wild

If you want to see the Hermit Crab in all its glory, and really learn about this species, then you have to see them in the wild. It is in the wild where Hermit Crabs truly shine. You can see them at their best and they are fascinating to watch.

There are two ways that you can experience and see Hermit Crabs in the wild. The first one is by watching documentaries. There are several documentaries about the Hermit Crab in the wild.

A great place to start is the BBC. The BBC has documentaries about the Hermit Crab and they are brilliant TV. If you don't want to watch a full documentary or haven't got the time to watch a full documentary, then pop on over to YouTube.

YouTube is a great place to find lots of videos about the Hermit Crab. You can find videos about the Hermit Crab on YouTube which are only a couple of minutes long. A quick and fun way to learn and watch Hermit Crabs.

It's a good idea to watch as much footage of Hermit Crabs as you can. Not only are Hermit Crabs an entertaining watch, it will also teach you about the Hermit Crab.

If you are going to have a Hermit Crab as a pet, then learning as much about them is essential. You can learn about them through clips on YouTube or documentaries - it's a fun and quick way to learn about Hermit Crabs.

There is one other way that you can see Hermit Crabs in the wild, and that is to experience them first hand in the wild. To do this, you can go to a nearby beach. If you are living in the Americas, Europe or Australia, then there is a good chance of seeing them.

If you are going to go to the beach to look for Hermit Crabs, this can be a fun activity. The best place to look for Hermit Crabs on the beach is in rock pools. Rock pools are one of the Hermit Crabs favourite places to rest and hide. This is a fun activity that can be done in groups.

There are local wildlife groups which have rock pool activities. It's a great way to experience wild animals in rock pools, not just the Hermit Crab.

Have a look at your local wildlife conservation group, especially the sea or marine conservation groups and see if there are any activities or groups in your area, or nearby. It's a great way to learn and experience wildlife and make some new friends at the same time.

When you are near a rock pool at the beach, you will probably find other sea creatures. Common rock pool marine animals are crabs, star fish and jelly fish.

If you are part of a group, follow the leader's advice on how to experience these animals. They are trained and know what they are doing.

If you see a Hermit Crab in a rock pool, they might try and protect themselves from you, by hiding inside their shell. Hermit Crabs will protect themselves from humans and other animals more often than not.

There are around 1000 different species of Hermit Crab. These 1000 different Hermit Crabs will sometimes face similar threats from the same animals. And sometimes they will face threats from the same animals in the wild.

The difference in species of Hermit Crab will also determine how the Hermit Crab protects itself from predators. And also what type of shell the Hermit Crab will use in order to protect itself.

If the Hermit Crab steals a shell in order to hide in that shell, then the shell they steal will depend upon what their environment and habitat is and where they are in the world.

So, what species of wild animals do Hermit Crabs protect themselves from? We are going to take a look at the species that Hermit Crabs protect themselves from in the wild.

Firstly, we are going to look at the species of wild animals that eat the Hermit Crab onshore. Onshore, Hermit Crabs are usually hunted and eaten by different types of bird species. These bird species range from seagulls and crows. However, they can also be vulnerable to other species.

Hermit Crabs can also be vulnerable to different species of mammals while onshore. Mammals such as raccoons will eat Hermit Crabs. Raccoons are not found everywhere in the wild. The Hermit Crabs that will be eaten by raccoons will be in North America.

Threats Towards Hermit Crabs

Being hunted and eaten by other animals is one of the threats posed to Hermit Crabs. Another threat posed to Hermit Crabs is from other Hermit Crabs. The last two threats towards Hermit Crabs are to do with the threats posed to Hermit Crabs by humans.

Hermit Crabs face two major threats from humans. The first threat is in being caught in trawler fishing nets. Many animals which are caught in fishing nets are not consumed by humans, while some are.

Sometimes Hermit Crabs are caught through fishing nets by mistake – at other times, they are caught deliberately.

Hermit Crabs are not usually eaten by people in Western countries. Therefore, if they are caught in the seas of Western countries, it is usually by mistake. However, in tropical areas of the world, Hermit Crabs are caught deliberate and eaten. This poses a threat to the Hermit Crab.

The Hermit Crab faces many threats while in the wild.

While at sea, or on the sea bed, Hermit Crabs are exposed to different threats, different species of wild animals.

Marine animals including fish like gunnels and clingfish also hunt and eat wild Hermit Crabs. They are also hunted and eaten by marine animals such as sea stars, snail-fish and larger crabs.

Hermit Crabs being eaten by larger crabs is not unusual. Hermit Crabs are not only eaten by larger crabs, they are also eaten by other Hermit Crabs. Clearly, Hermit Crabs can also be cannibals - they will eat their own kind.

Hermit Crabs Protecting Themselves

As Hermit Crabs face many natural predators in the wild, it is only natural that they will protect themselves from these predators.

The Hermit Crabs will protect themselves by stealing the shells of other animals and hide in those shells.

Hermit Crabs will often change their shells, depending on their size and maturity. As the Hermit Crab grows older and matures, they will need new and bigger shells to hide under.

This is when they are most vulnerable to being attacked by other animals when they float from one shell to another, they become exposed and risk being eaten by other animals.

Hermit Crabs will protect themselves from other animals by stealing shells at the bottom of the ocean. Although, they also can and will steal the shells of other animals to protect themselves on beaches, it depends on the species of Hermit Crab and where they come from.

The biggest challenge that any Hermit Crab will face is from predators. They live a daily survival battle, like most other wild animals. One mistake can be the end of a Hermit Crabs life. Therefore, they will do everything they can to protect themselves from other animals.

A final way that Hermit Crabs will protect themselves from other animals is by pinching those who try and attack them. Hermit Crabs have claws or pincers for this reason; it is a defence mechanism which can help them ward off predators or attackers.

Now that we know what eats Hermit Crabs, let us look at what Hermit Crabs eat in the wild.

Chapter 3. What Hermit Crabs Eat

As we have already observed earlier in the book, Hermit Crabs will eat almost anything that they can get their hands on. From dead animals to plant-based food, Hermit Crabs will eat it. Hermit Crabs are also cannibalistic - they are known to eat other Hermit Crabs.

You can call the diet of a Hermit Crab many things. They are meat eaters, they are plant eaters, they are cannibals and they are scavengers. If anything, the Hermit Crab will eat almost anything.

The Hermit Crab is not a fussy eater in the wild. They are opportunistic eaters. Basically, the Hermit Crab will feast upon anything they stumble upon. It doesn't really matter to them what it is.

This is a great survival tool for the Hermit Crab. By not being fussy about what they eat, Hermit Crabs do not limit themselves to what is available to them in terms of food. If you are looking to survive, it is a great strategy.

It also shows us just how resilient these little crabs are. They may be small, but they are survivors. Survivors who take advantage of their surroundings, especially their surroundings in terms of food supply.

The good news for Hermit Crabs in captivity as pets is that they don't have to go and hunt for food or worry about food. It will always be supplied to them by you, which helps them to avoid worrying about finding food.

But, if you are looking to keep a Hermit Crab as a pet, you might want to know what you should feed it. The Hermit Crab can eat many things in captivity - you can even feed him foods that he wouldn't find in his natural habitat, such as various vegetables.

The Hermit Crab isn't a conventional pet so finding food specifically made for the Hermit Crab can be difficult to find. However, it's not impossible to feed it.

You can find pet Hermit Crab food in your local pet store. If you are going to buy your Hermit Crab food in this way, then you should go to one of the larger pet stores. The bigger pet stores have more in them and cover a wider variety of animal supplies, than smaller pet stores.

If you can't find hermit Crab food in a bigger pet store, then go online and buy it that way. You can find specialized Hermit Crab food on sites like Amazon and it's pretty cheap too.

Besides eating specialized Hermit Crab food, they can also eat a variety of other things. Such as vegetables or fruit.

When you get your new pet Hermit Crab, you will be wondering 'What food do Hermit Crabs eat?', 'What should I feed my new pet Hermit Crab?'. Here, we are going to give you an answer to both of those questions.

Before we get into what you should feed your pet Hermit Crab, let us take a look at what they eat in the wild. So, what do Hermit Crabs eat in the wild? Let us take a look at what Hermit Crabs eat in the wild.

What Hermit Crabs Eat In The Wild

There are many things that Hermit Crabs will eat while in the wild. As you know, Hermit Crabs will eat just about anything they come across.

What a Hermit Crab will eat in the wild, will depend on whether the Hermit Crab is eating on land, or, whether they are eating in the ocean.

There is an obvious reason for this of course. Different types of food will be available to the Hermit Crabs on land and in the ocean.

Therefore, there is a difference between what they will eat while on land, and what they will eat while in the ocean.

At the same time though, sometimes they will eat the same things on land as in the ocean. As things such as animals and sea weed can wash ashore.

While on land, the Hermit Crab will eat various things. Their diet can be very different on land, than what they eat in the ocean.

This is because of the foods available to them on land, compared to the foods available to them while in the ocean. There are certain foods that they eat on land, which is not available to them while they are in the ocean.

These foods are mainly foods from trees or land plants. The foods that Hermit Crabs will typically eat while on land are as follows: they will eat various plants on land, they will eat grass on land, and, Hermit Crabs will also eat things such as fallen fruit and deadwood from trees.

Their diet is different while they are in the ocean. Hermit Crabs while in the ocean will eat a wide range of things. These things include things such as plants and dead animals. Hermit Crabs aren't fussy about what they eat - they are opportunists, scavengers which will eat anything. You can buy your Hermit Crabs food in your local pet store.

What You Should Feed Your Pet

There are two types of ways that you can feed your Hermit Crab, both of these methods are advised. The first way you should feed your Hermit Crab, is with specialized Hermit Crab food, which can be found in pet stores. The second way you can feed your Hermit Crab is with foods that you can buy out of your local store. Hermit Crabs can eat foods such as vegetables and nuts.

You should feed your pet Hermit Crab specialized food because it will give him the proper nutrition he needs. The specialized Hermit Crab food offers a healthy and nutritional diet for the Hermit Crab.

You should be feeding your Hermit Crab on a daily basis. In other words, it is important for you to give your Hermit Crab some of his specialized food daily. A fresh supply on a daily basis should be provided, while you disregard any let over food from the previous day.

You should never leave food lying around too long in your Hermit Crabs tank. This is an unhealthy practice and can be a breeding ground for bacteria which could make your Hermit Crab unwell, or even prove fatal.

Chapter 4. Where To Get started

In the first few chapters of this book, you have learned all about the Hermit Crab in the wild. You have learned about what a Hermit Crab is and that they are a marine animal that lives in both the ocean and on land.

You have also learned about their appearance and the different species of Hermit Crab. As well as their behaviour in the wild; such as their behaviours in eating and avoiding predators. Learning all about the Hermit Crab in the wild, is a good foundation for getting to know the Hermit Crab. It is encouraged that you should learn as much about the Hermit Crab as you possibly can, before you buy your own Hermit Crab as a pet. Learning all about Hermit Crabs is easy.

There are various ways to learn about your Hermit Crab. Read books about the Hermit Crabs. Watch documentaries and video clips about Hermit Crabs. And finally, if you can, it is a great learning experience if you can get up close and personal with Hermit Crabs in the wild.

Once you have learned all about the Hermit Crab, you will now have a good understanding of the Hermit Crab.

Now that you have a good understanding of what a Hermit Crab is, you will want to know where to get started. So, how do you start on your adventure to having a cute Hermit Crab for a pet?

In this chapter, we are going to take a step-by-step guide to how you can get started on your journey to getting a pet Hermit Crab and looking after one as a pet.

Guidelines To Getting Started

Like having any other new pet that you are unfamiliar with having, buying and starting a new life with a Hermit Crab can be a little daunting, but also exciting!

To get started on owning and having your own Hermit Crab as a pet, take on board these guidelines:

▪ ***Do Some Research***

Firstly, before you even buy your pet crab, you will want to do some research about Hermit Crabs, specifically, you should learn about pet Hermit Crabs.

This book is an excellent foundation for that, as you've learned about Hermit Crabs in the wild and will go onto learning about pet Hermit Crabs.

You should also learn as much about Hermit Crabs in the wild, as you can. Learning about Hermit Crabs in the wild can give you a good idea about what Hermit Crabs are like. Specifically what their personality is like.

Also, do some research about what you will need to buy for your new pet Hermit Crab.

▪ ***Buy What You Need***

Once you have learned about Hermit Crabs, you will next need to figure out what kind of Hermit Crab you want. As we have said, there are about 1000 different types of species of Hermit Crab.

Although all of these species are not up for sale as pets, there are many different species of Hermit Crab, you will need to buy items which as specifically for your Hermit Crab.

Luckily that is not as hard as it seems. There are only two main types of Hermit Crabs which are sold as pets – as I mentioned earlier in this book. Therefore, it should be very straight forward and simple to buy the items and food for your pet.

Decide on what type of Hermit Crab you want. The next step after this is to buy your equipment, which is suitable for the species of Hermit Crab you have chosen to buy.

Most of the equipment that you will buy is the same for any species of Hermit Crab. The only difference is the size of the tan. Make sure the tank is suitable for the size of your new Hermit Crab.

You will need to know which of the two species of Hermit Crab you want to buy, before you buy the equipment for your Hermit Crab. Then you can buy the suitable equipment afterwards.

The best advice that we can give you is to buy your Hermit Crab and his equipment on the same day. This will make it easier for you.

There are several items which are essential when you are buying your Hermit Crab. These essential items are things that the Hermit Crab cannot live without. So, when buying things for your Hermit Crab, you shouldn't leave these things out - such as a tank.
A tank is essential for your new Hermit Crab. There are different types of Hermit Crab tanks that you can get, such as an aquarium tank or a marine terrarium.

Whichever tank you choose, make sure that it is big enough for your pet Hermit Crab and make sure that it is a strong tank. A strong tank is essential because you are going to have to put sand inside it.

The tank you buy has to be strong and sturdy. You don't want your tank to fall over easily, as this can cause accidents or harm your crab. If your tank doesn't come supplied with its own stand, then, it's important for you to find a stand which is sturdy enough for the tank to fit on.

A good idea is to put it on a wooden desk top, or something equivalent to that. If you don't want to spend a lot of money on it, then you can buy one for a bargain from Amazon. Just make sure that the weight of the tank can be supported by the desk.

Remember, you are going to have to fill the tank up with sand - that means that the tank is going to be heavier than when you purchased it. Therefore, the tank needs something strong to support it.

Putting sand at the base of your tank is another essential for your Hermit Crab.

Before you put your sand in the tank, make sure that you put something underneath it, such as paper to line it - doing this can make it easier to clean out when you get around to cleaning.

Also, make sure that all the edges are securely covered - make sure that there is no way that the crab can get out and that the crab will be secure in its new home.

Also, make sure that air can get in your tank so that the air can circulate throughout. Although you want to make sure that the tank is secure that your Hermit Crab won't get out, you will also want to make sure that your Hermit Crab can breathe - which means that you want to make sure that enough air can get in your tank. A lid with aeration holes is therefore essential.

Make sure that your sand is wet - that the sand it is moist. Then, add some safe sea salt. The safe sea salt is specifically designed for animals such as Hermit Crabs. You will also want to put some water-conditioning fluids in the tank. Make sure that the amount you put in is safe and follow the guides.

If you are not sure, ask your local pet shop (or ask the person who you are buying the Hermit Crab from).

- ***What to put in the tank***

The sand should be about 15cm - that is deep enough. You will want to add different things in the tank for your Hermit Crab.

These are the following things that you will want to put in your tank for your Hermit Crab: a water dish (so your Hermit Crab can drink), a food dish (so your Hermit Crab can eat), some shells (so that your Hermit Crab can hide), a Hermit Crab hidey hut (so that your Hermit Crab can hide or sleep).

There are other things that you should put in your tank, to help your Hermit Crab. Other things that you should put in your tank are things such as rocks and branches so that your Hermit Crab can climb and have an activity to do.

Also you can include moss and extra sponges as this helps soak up excess moisture.

A Hermit Crab's tank shouldn't be clogged up with stuff. You shouldn't put so many toys and dishes in the tank that the Hermit Crab can't move about in freely. The Hermit Crab needs plenty of room to move about in.

As your Hermit Crab will need plenty of room to move about in, you should keep this in mind when you are buying the tank itself. You shouldn't buy a tank which is too small for the Hermit Crab.

You will also want to watch your Hermit Crab running around and playing. You can only see him clearly running about or playing in his tank if his tank is clean.

Here is a list of some of the essential items that you will need for your Hermit Crab in his tank. Three dishes, one for fresh water, one for salt water and one for his food.

You will also need a place where he can hide, such as a log. And, you can even put inside the tank a plant or two along with a few toys.

There are also things that you should avoid putting in your tank. Avoid putting in anything breakable, this includes dishes. Try to use plastic ones. Avoid putting any harmful chemicals in the tank; only wash the tank and equipment with hot water.

Take this advice on board when you are setting up his tank (crabbit).

- ***Setting Up The Crabbit***

Now that you know the steps that you need to take to set up the crabbit (the crabbit is the home tank of your new pet Hermit Crab), in other words, what you should and shouldn't put in your tank, you will now want to get started in setting up the crabbit tank.

When you have bought all of your equipment, setting up your crabbit is really simple. It shouldn't take you that long to set up the crabbit, probably about a half an hour or so. The most challenging part of setting up your crabbit, is putting in the sand.

To get started, you will need your tank in front of it.

Before you start setting your tank up, you will want to ask yourself a few of these questions. 'Where am I going to put the tank?' 'Where in your living space is suitable for the tank?'

When asking yourself these questions, keep in mind the following. Choose somewhere that is not too hot or too cold. You should never put your tank up against a heater, radiator, window or door.

If you do, your Hermit Crab will be vulnerable. These places, especially radiators and windows, can have a climate which changes easily. They can expose Hermit Crabs to temperatures which are too hot or too cold.

The temperature is one of the most important things for Hermit Crabs. They need the temperature to be the right temperature. Too hot and it could kill your Hermit Crab. Too cold and it can also kill your Hermit Crab.

Setting the right temperature for your Hermit Crab is of the utmost importance. The temperature should be around 72F. That is a good temperature for the Hermit Crab, as it is a humid enough temperature.

A reptile aquarium is suitable for Hermit Crabs. It is suitable because it is about the right size for Hermit Crabs and it is built with animals in mind.

Your size of tank should depend upon how many Hermit Crabs you are getting as pets. If you are getting a Hermit Crab, it's best to buy a mate for your Hermit Crab.

In other words, it's best to buy at least two Hermit Crabs, as Hermit Crabs are social animals. This is especially true if you are looking to breed Hermit Crabs.

A word of warning though : sometimes, animals can fight, no matter what type of species the animal is. This is particularly true of animals which are of the same sex, as they can become territorial and competitive.

Therefore, you will want to make sure that your two pet Hermit Crabs get on well before you get them. Who you buy the Hermit Crabs off of will know if the two crabs get on well with one another.

How will you know they get on well? You can know that your two new Hermit Crabs get on well by asking the person who you are buying them off if they get on well. See what they say about the crabs.

Buying two Hermit Crabs can also save you money in the long run, if you breed the crabs. Hermit Crabs don't live that long in captivity, only about a year. Compared with around 20 years in the wild.

Because they don't live that long in the wild, you will have to buy a Hermit Crab on a yearly basis, if you want to keep having a Hermit Crab. To avoid this, it's best to breed them. That way you won't have to buy any more.

When preparing your crabbit, make sure that you keep the crabbit humid. You will also want to keep in mind the air; make sure that there is enough air circulating the crabbit so that the Hermit Crab or Hermit Crabs can breathe.

- ***Make Sure The Hermit Crab Is Humid***

Making sure that the environment is humid in your home and your tank is important for Hermit Crabs breeding, it is also important for Hermit Crabs in general. Hermit Crabs cannot and will not survive without a humid temperature.

Therefore, make sure that you keep your Hermit Crabs crabbit is humid. To keep the tank humid, you will want to buy something called a humidity gauge. By installing or keeping a humidity gauge in your crabbit, you will keep your tank at the correct humidity level.

You will be able to either buy a humidity gauge in your local pet store or online in stores such as Amazon. Buy it when you are buying all of your other equipment for your crab - it will save you time and a second journey to the pet store.

It is important to make sure that your crabbit is humid enough. There needs to be plenty of humidity for Hermit Crabs because Hermit Crabs cannot breathe properly unless the air is humid enough. The air needs to be humid for Hermit Crabs because they breathe through their gills, and this method of respiration requires moisture.

When making sure that the air is humid enough for your Hermit Crab, you will want to make sure that the temperature in mind. Keep in mind that the humidity should not be below 70%, a good humidity rate for Hermit Crabs is around 75%. If it is below 70%, then they will suffocate and die. Therefore, it is very important to keep the air humid enough for them.

What is worse about it is that the Hermit Crabs will not die right away if the air is not humid enough. It can be a very painful death for them which can last weeks or months. To look after your pet Hermit Crab and make sure that you avoid this from happening, keep the humidity level at 75%.

- ***How To Keep Your Tank Humid***

A great way to keep your tank humid for your Hermit Crab is to put moss in the crabbit tank. That is why you were advised earlier in the book to put moss in the tank.

The moss helps and will help keep your tank humid. The Hermit Crabs will also eat the moss that you put in the tank. This is okay and is nothing to worry about. You will be able to buy moss at your local pet store, or in online pet stores. If you can't get moss, then a good alternative is to use sponges. Although, moss is best. You can simply spray the moss or sponges gently with a mister/spray bottle to increase moisture levels.

- ***The Temperature Of Your Tank***

Next, make sure that you keep your tank at the right temperature. You might want to keep your tank away from any heaters and put the tank against a plain wall without heaters. This is because heaters can end up being too hot and may over heat the tank. Which will either create discomfort, or mean that the Hermit Crab will die. Therefore, you want to avoid it at all costs.

A good idea is to keep a thermometer in your tank. Make sure that it is out of reach from your pet Hermit Crab, so attaching it on the side of the tank will work well. What temperature should you keep your tank in? You will want to make sure that the tank stays at around 75 to 80 degrees Fahrenheit.

Hermit Crabs are usually found in tropical climates all across the world. Therefore, you will want to make sure that your tank stays at this temperature. It replicates the sort of temperature that they would be used to in their natural surroundings.

If the tank is not kept at a correct temperature, then the Hermit Crab can have lots of problems happen to it. Problems such as losing limbs, over exhaustion and even death. It's very unhealthy to keep your crab at a temperature too hot or too cold.

- ***Line Your Tank With Sand***

Before you put your Hermit Crab inside the tank, you will want to line the tank with sand.

You cannot put just any sand inside the tank. You will have to make sure that it is sand which is suitable for your Hermit Crab. The sand which is suitable for your Hermit Crab is called arrogate sand.

Other sands will be harmful to your pet Hermit Crab. This is because other sands are too rough for the Hermit Crab. As the Hermit Crab has a sensitive and soft body, they can easily be hurt by other sand, because it is simply too rough for them.

Play sand should be avoided. Play sand can have harmful chemicals put in them, which could either hurt your crab or make the crab severely ill. It can even result in death. Therefore, avoid play sand. You should buy your sand out of a pet store, where the sand will be the correct sand for your Hermit Crab.

- ***Substrate For The Crabbit***

When you put the sand into your crabbit tank, you will also want to put inside the tank something called “substrate”. Substrate helps keep the tank moist and humid. The proper substrate is essential for your pet Hermit Crab’s survival in the tank.

Your tank should be at least deep enough for around ten gallons of sand. The sand should be deep for Hermit Crabs. In the wild, Hermit Crabs will dig underground. They will want to do the same and need to do the same while in their tank. This replicates their natural environment and behaviour.

The Hermit Crabs will bury themselves underneath the sand for a few reasons. In the wild, it can be a good place to be, if you are wanting to avoid predators like a Hermit Crab does. Another reason they bury themselves underneath the sand is that it is dark. The Hermit Crab prefers the darkness - it is, after all, a nocturnal animal. Escaping underneath the sand and into the darkness also helps these animals to sleep.

There is one final biological reason why they bury themselves underneath the sand. They also bury themselves underneath the sand because the darkness helps bring out a chemical in their body called ecdysone. Ecdysone helps the Hermit Crab shed their skin. They could not shed their skin without it.

While underneath the sand, the Hermit Crab will shed their excess skin, also known as their exoskeleton skin. Shedding their exoskeleton skin makes them extremely vulnerable to predators. Going underneath the sand protects them.

Although as a pet you will not have to worry about predators, the behaviour will still occur in the Hermit Crab, because it is in their nature. But, you do have to worry about the sand.

This is why it is important to have the right type of sand and to keep the sand moist. While the Hermit Crabs are underneath the sand, they can become dehydrated without moist sand. The moist sand allows them to stay hydrated.

There is one final ingredient to keep your tank moist. The final ingredient to keeping your tank moist is that you use coconut fibre. Coconut fibre helps keep the sand moist for your Hermit Crab. When you put coconut fibre into the sand, you retain the water which is in the sand. This, in turn, helps the Hermit Crabs stay dehydrated.

The Hermit Crab can stay buried under ground for a long time once they are shedding their skin. Particularly the bigger Hermit Crabs. The bigger Hermit Crabs, the longer they will stay buried underneath the sand, which makes it even more important to have moist sand.

The bigger Hermit Crabs can stay under ground for up to three months. They can stay underneath the sand for up to three months while they are shedding their skin. Therefore, don't worry if your Hermit Crab does this, it's completely normal. Although you may wish to check on it from time to time to ensure all is well.

If in any doubt about what sand you should use for your Hermit Crabs credit, or what materials and products to use in the credit, ask your local pet store. They will be able to show you the correct equipment that you need and also sell you the correct equipment for your new pet Hermit Crab.

- ***Amount Of Substrate***

Now that you know what sand to put in your crabbit and that you will need to put substrate in your crab, you will want to know, 'How many substrates should I put in it?' That is a good question. You should definitely measure the amount of substrate that you put into your crabbit.

The amount of substrate that you put in your crabbit is important for your Hermit Crab. How big your Hermit Crab is will determine the amount of substrate that you need to put in the crabbit. You should roughly put about 4 or 5 times as much substrate in your tank, as the height of your Hermit Crab.

This is important. As we have said before, Hermit Crabs will need to bury underneath the sand, so they will need plenty of room. Therefore, the right amount of substrate is important for this species. The substrate is very helpful for the Hermit Crab.

It can help them do many things that they could not do without the substrate. This includes things such as digging underneath the sand to make and build caves and burrows. The caves that the Hermit Crab builds, helps them to hide underneath the sand; it gives them a place to live and sleep underneath the sand too.

- ***When To Change Your Substrate***

You will want to keep changing your substrate every four or five months. Changing your substrate every four or five months helps to keep the tank clean. It keeps your Hermit Crabs environment clean and germ-free. If you don't change the substrate, then, not only will your Hermit Crab not have somewhere clean and tiny to stay, but, it can and will and also make the Hermit Crab unwell.

Think of it like you would if you had any other pet, such as a hamster or a rabbit. You would clean your hamster's cage or your rabbit's hutch often. You would clean them often so that the environment your pet hamster or pet rabbit in is clean and relatively free of bacteria and odours. But, you would also make sure the cage or hut is clean to avoid any diseases happening. Or, making them feel unwell.

If you don't clean the crabbit our or don't change the substrate often, you will risk the same things for your pet Hermit Crab. What's more, if the substrate is not changed often, then the substrate will start to go mouldy.

Again, this creates an unhealthy environment for your pet Hermit Crab and could affect their health.

What you should do is keep an eye on your Hermit Crabs sand and substrate. Check it every three weeks to make sure that it is healthy and not getting mouldy. If you see it beginning to get mouldy, then you should immediately replace it. If not, then check it again in another few weeks and if it needs changing then, change it.

- ***Cleaning Your Equipment***

You should clean out your crabbit equipment regularly. What is your equipment? Your equipment is things such as feeding bowls and water bowls. Or, any hand made things which are in the crabbit, such as places where the Hermit Crab hides.

How often should you clean your equipment? With things such as food trays or water bowls, you should be cleaning these out on a daily basis. Food can get stale and water can become warm and unclean very quickly. Therefore, cleaning out your pet Hermit Crab's food and water bowls on a daily basis is essential.

Try not to put in more food than you need each day. This will avoid food wastage or food becoming mouldy and breeding bacteria, causing illness and bad odours.

Try to sterilise your dishes, shells and other equipment on a weekly basis.

Don't sterilise them with any harmful chemicals. Some freshly boiled water should be enough. You can leave the dishes to steep in the hot water, then give them a good clean out. Dry them and put them back inside the crabbit with some fresh food and water.

Giving the bowls, dishes, shells and other equipment a good clean, by sterilising them, is a great way to keep your Hermit Crabs crabbit healthy. It will ensure that things such as diseases and moulds are kept at bay. Healthy equipment is as essential as healthy sand.

If your Hermit Crab does not have access to clean healthy food and water on a regular basis, then, it can make the Hermit Crab unwell. The last thing that you want is to give your Hermit Crab food that has been lying for days or water that has been lying for days.

Once you have cleaned and dried the equipment, make sure that you leave the equipment to cool down. Give it plenty of time to cool down, perhaps about an hour, before you put it back into the crabbit. This ensures that your Hermit Crab will not be hurt by the warm equipment or spoil any clean water/food.

- ***Hiding Places For Your Hermit Crab***

You will want to make sure that your Hermit Crab has places to hide in their crabbit. It is in a Hermit Crabs natural behaviour to hide in things. Usually, in the wild, they will hide in things such as shells. Shells are the usual places that Hermit Crabs will hide under. When setting up your crabbit, put some shells in there.

The size of your shells will depend on the size of your Hermit Crab. The shells should and must be bigger than the Hermit Crab - this allows the Hermit Crabs to hide within the shells. You should also take into consideration how many Hermit Crabs you have. The more Hermit Crabs you have, the more shells that you will need in your tank.

The shells, like other equipment you put in the crabbit, such as plants, rocks or tree branches, can help your Hermit Crab to feel safe and secure. It gives your Hermit Crab somewhere to hide, which makes them feel less vulnerable and more secure. Make sure that these items are clean.

Ensure that you don't put anything in that could harm the Hermit Crab. Don't put in things in the crabbit which could break easily, as this could hurt the Hermit Crab. The best type of material to put in the crabbit is a strong plastic. Although, using coconut shells as a place for them to hide, can also be a very good idea.

Installing plants in your Hermit Crab are also a very good idea. Plants replicate the Hermit Crabs natural environment and make the crabbit feel like home for the Hermit Crab. Ensure that you put the right plants inside the Hermit Crab. You will want to avoid plants which could be harmful or poisonous to your Hermit Crab. If you are in doubt, ask your local pet store.

Ideally, you will want to put plants into your Hermit Crab which they would be surrounded with in their natural environment. Put real plants inside the Hermit Crab's crabbit. Avoid putting plants in which are synthetic or plastic.

Synthetic and plastic plants are unnatural and therefore can be harmful to your Hermit Crab. Plastic or synthetic plants are usually made with chemicals. These chemicals can be harmful and dangerous for your pet Hermit Crab if your Hermit Crab digests them. Keep them out of reach from your Hermit Crab.

Not only are these type of plants harmful to the Hermit Crab, they also don't look as nice as real plants. Real plants look better and offer a more natural environment for your crab. The key to having a Hermit Crab is to try and replicate its natural environment as much as possible.

Hermit Crabs can also be like toddlers - a bit destructive at times! Although still adorable, they can and will eat plants. So, it is extremely important not to place any plants within the crabbit which might poison them. When you put in your plants, be prepared for them not lasting.

Often, as Hermit Crabs will eat the plants, the plants will not last. Either, the plants will regrow and blossom again, or, you will have to buy more plants for them to put in your Hermit Crab. You may want to try and buy plants in bulk if you can.

Buying your plants in bulk can help save money for you. Buying in bulk costs less in the long run than buying plants individually. If you are buying them in bulk, you will have to look after the plants too before using them as replacements within the tank. Keep the plants in a safe place - avoid keeping them outside and keep the plants somewhere indoors.

- ***Food And Water***

Once you have prepared the crabbit and set it all up, you will next want to put in your food and water for the crab. Your Hermit Crab will need access to food and water on a daily basis. Below we are going to show you what type of water you will need and what type of food you will need for your pet Hermit Crab. Let's start with water first.

Like all animals, water is essential for the survival of the Hermit Crab. Without water, the Hermit Crab will not survive. It is essential that you provide your Hermit Crab with two types of water. The first type of water that you want to provide for your Hermit Crab is normal fresh water. The second type of water that you will want to provide for your Hermit Crab is sea water (or salt water).

You should have two separate water dishes for your pet crab. One of the water dishes is where you should put the normal fresh water. The other dish is where you should put the salt water. Don't mix these two glasses of water together in the one dish. Providing your pet crab with both of these types of water is important.

Make sure that the salt water and fresh water dishes that you provide for your Hermit Crab is not too deep. Make sure that they are shallow so that your Hermit Crab can get out of the dishes if he happens to fall in. Water dishes which are a centimetre or two in depth should do the job. Just make sure that the dishes are easily accessible, both in terms of the Hermit Crab having easy access to drinking the water and easy access to getting out of the dish, if he happens to fall in.

You can buy freshwater easily. It should be available in any local store or pet store. With salt water or sea water, you most likely won't find it in your local store. You might even have difficulty finding it in your local pet store. However, larger pet stores or specialised online pet stores will have salt water available.

Make sure that you use salt water which is for Hermit Crabs. In other words, make sure that you do not use water which is made, packaged and processed for humans. The best idea is to buy your water, whether fresh water or salt water, which has been specifically made for the Hermit Crab, or has been recommended for species such as this.

Do not create your own salt water. What we mean by this is, do not put salt into fresh water and then give it to your pet Hermit Crab. This is not a substitute for sea salt and can be particularly damaging to your Hermit Crabs. You will have to buy the proper stuff; proper sea salt water.

The size of your dishes and the depth of the water in the dishes should depend upon the size of your Hermit Crab. As you know, there are different species of Hermit Crab. Some Hermit Crabs are bigger than others. Some will need more water provided to them than others. Some will also need an area where they can bathe in.

For example, some species of Hermit Crab like to submerge themselves in water. What matters is the type of species you have, whether it is a species which is a land based Hermit Crab or a marine based Hermit Crab. The type of species matters.

If you have a species of Hermit Crab which is naturally a land based Hermit Crab in the wild, then, a shallow dish is best. If the dish waters are too high, then the Hermit Crabs could drown, as they are not suited to a marine environment.

Whichever species of Hermit Crab you have, whether that species is a land species or a marine species, make sure you set up your water place with consideration. Make sure your Hermit Crab can easily access the water and get out of the water.

A good way to do this is to design your dish water area. Have places near the dish water which have things such as rocks, branches or logs, so that your Hermit Crab can climb out of the dish in case he falls in and wants to get back out again.

Another good idea for your water area is to try and get dishes or your water pool (if you set up one) to have sloping sides. The slopes provide an easy way for your Hermit Crab to get in and out. This can be a particularly good idea for marine based Hermit Crabs.

The sloped dishes act as both a deep water area and a shallow water area. The Hermit Crab can submerge itself in the deep end of the water. While, if the Hermit Crab is just looking for a drink, he can use the shallow end, without getting submerged.

Whatever you do, avoid putting tap water into your dishes. Tap water will kill your Hermit Crab, because of the chemicals - such as chlorine - which are deadly to Hermit Crabs. The water you should use shouldn't have any added chemicals to it.

This is why it is best to get water which is specifically provided for the Hermit Crab, provided by people who either specialise in pet supplies or specialise in marine pet supplies.

Once you have taken these steps, you have set up your Hermit Crabs crabbit. You should prepare the crabbit before you put your new pet Hermit Crab into it.

Setting up your Hermit Crab's crabbit is a fun experience. You will be making a new home for your Hermit Crab. You can also get a bit creative and design your crabbit in your own way. Put the plants where you want them, the hiding place where you want it and their dishes.

When you are setting up your crabbit, make sure that it is somewhere you can see it, as you will obviously want to observe your Hermit Crab. You could put your tank somewhere like opposite a living room chair. That can be an easy way for you to watch your Hermit Crab while you are chilling out.

Now that you've learned what a crabbit is, let us look at the essential equipment you will need for Hermit Crab, in the next chapter.

Chapter 5. Essential Equipment For Your Pet Crab

In this chapter, we are going to look at essential equipment that you will need for your pet crab. You are already familiar at this point to some of the equipment you will need for your pet Hermit Crab.

In this chapter, we are going to take an in-depth look at the equipment you will need for your pet Hermit Crab. First, let us take a look at the costs of keeping a Hermit Crab. This includes the weekly, monthly and one-off costs. Please note that costs mentioned in this book were correct at the time of going to press – and that prices can change due to currency fluctuations.. This is, of course, outside of our control.

The cost of keeping the Hermit Crab as a pet varies, depending on whether you are buying food and equipment for your Hermit Crab on a weekly or monthly basis. Buying the Hermit Crab itself will cost you between $2 to $45 (or £1.53 to £34.52).

The prices vary on buying Hermit Crabs because there are different species of Hermit Crabs. The species of Hermit Crab you buy will determine the price of the crab.

The cost of feeding your Hermit Crab varies too. The price of one bag of Hermit Crab food is between $4.25 and $5 (or £3.26 and £3.84). To buy these on a monthly basis would cost you $17 to $20 (or £13.04 to £15.34.) These prices are based up the website Hermitcrabpatch.com, based upon two food mixtures that you can buy from the website for Hermit Crabs. Please note that any references to websites were live at the time of writing this book and may change. This is obviously outside of our control.

Or, you could buy the Hermit Crabs food on Amazon. Buying Hermit Crab food on Amazon is roughly the same price. For example, a Hermit Crab food called 'Hikari Crab Cuisine' is $5 (or £3.99), you can buy a pack like this once a week for your crab. Which will cost you $20 (or £15.96).

Your average weekly Hermit Crab food should come to around $5 (or £3.84) based on the estimates of various Hermit Crab foods. Which is around $20 (or £15.34) per month.

The sand for your Hermit Crab will cost around $5.50 (which is £4.22). And the substrate will cost you around $13 (which is £9.97). You won't need to buy the sand or the substrate as much as food. Weekly it will cost you around $18.50 (or £14.19) a week for both of them. That is $74 (or £56.77) on a monthly basis.

You can buy your water from Pet Smart. The fresh water from Pet Smart is $8.29 (or £6.36), on a weekly basis. And, $33.16 (or £25.44) on a monthly basis. Whereas, you can buy salt water in places such as Complete Aquatics for $23.81 (or £18.27), which will do you on a monthly basis. This comes in at $5.95 (or, £4.56) on a weekly basis.

Finally, if you want to save money, you can buy Hermit Crabs their equipment and food in a larger kit. This larger kit comes with everything that you need, including sand, water, food, shells, at the Hermit Crab Patch website. This will cost you $63.75 (or £48.90).

The average cost of keeping a Hermit Crab a week is $42.49 (or, £32.59), and the monthly average keep of a Hermit Crab is $169.96 (which is £130.38. This includes all of the essentials; food, water, substrate and sand. Whereas, your one off payment for buying the Hermit Crab is between $2 and $45 (or £1.53 to £34.52). And the one off payment for the tank is around $39.09 (which is £29.99), which can be bought from Amazon.

Like all pets, Hermit Crabs need their own special equipment. There are many things that you will have to buy your pet crab before you actually buy the crab itself. You want to prepare where the crab is going to stay in your house or apartment before you buy the crab and bring your new pet home.

In the last chapter, we showed you a step-by-step guide of how you can set up your own crabbit. And introduced you to some of the equipment that you will need for your pet Hermit Crab.

There are several things that the Hermit Crab needs in their crabbit. These things are the essential equipment that you will need to put into your crabbit for the Hermit Crab. The essential equipment for your Hermit Crab that we are going to talk about, is equipment that you are highly advised to buy.

Buying for your new Hermit Crab can be a lot of fun. There is a lot to buy and you are buying them to make your Hermit Crabs crabbit a better and happier place for your Hermit Crab. So, what is the essential equipment that you will need for your new pet? Here is the essential equipment that you will need.

- ***Sand***

Putting sand into your tank is the first important step for your Hermit Crab. The sand is at the core of your crabbit and therefore, the most important element of the crabbit. You cannot set up a crabbit without the sand. The sand of the crabbit is the essential ingredient.

- ***Build A Hiding Place***

A place where your Hermit Crab can hide and sleep is a perfect idea for your Hermit Crab. There are several ways that you can create a hiding place for your crab. This includes things such as using wood, or drift wood, so that your Hermit Crab can hide underneath.

There are lots of ways that you can create a hidden gem for your Hermit Crab. Think of it as creating a bed and a bedroom for your Hermit Crab.

Use things such as wood, rocks and coconuts as a place of shelter and security for your crab.

Keep in mind that it should be a secure hiding place - a hiding place that doesn't cave in or fall easily, but one which is established in the crabbit securely. You should design the hidden place so that there is a room in the middle where the Hermit Crab can access. But one that has a roof, side and back.

Think of it as a hidden cave. Try and replicate a cave-like hidden place for your pet Hermit Crab. And they will be happy and secure with it.

- ***Rocks, Plants and Sea Shells***

The next essential things for your Hermit Crab are rocks plants and sea shells. You don't need to go out into nature and collect either rocks or sea shells, you can purchase these from your local pet store, or online. With plants, you can do the same.

As we have said before, make sure that you put the right plants into your crabbit. If the plants are poisonous, then it can be very harmful to your pet. So, what are the types of plants you should put in your crabbit?

The great news is, there is a long list of plants that you can put into your crabbit. Plants which will be suitable for your tank and your Hermit Crab.

These are just some of the species of plants that you can put into your crabbit:

1) Air Plants
2) Camilla
3) Dandelion
4) Daisies
5) Reeds
6) Spider plants

These are just some of the more popular plants that you can put into your crabbit. There are a lot more. You don't need to put all of these plants in your crabbit. One or two could do, or even just one of these plants will be good.

You will have to plant one of these plants within your crabbit. Make sure that you plant it securely, deep enough so that the plant is not uprooted easily. To plant your plant, follow some of these basic and easy steps:

- ***Dig A Hole***

Digging a hole in your sand is the first step towards planting your plant in your crabbit. To do this, use a small trowel. Your trowel should be long enough that you will only need to dig down and scope out the sand once.

Use your own judgement when digging the hole. To give you a good guidance on it, you should be placing the plant in a hole where the roots of the plant are securely underneath the sand.

- ***Put Your Plant Inside***

Before you put the plant inside, first measure it against the hole.
If the plant fits well into the hole, it's time to take the next step. The next step is to put your soil in the hole. The best type of soil for this is organic soil. Avoid using soils which have any type of pesticides or chemicals within it.

- ***Use Some Organic Soil***

Using an organic soil will help you avoid harmful chemicals which could harm your Hermit Crab. First, put some of the soil at the bottom of the hole. Then, when you have done this, put the plant in the hole and hold the plant with one hand.

While doing this, take more of the soil and put it inside the hole. Make sure that the plant has soil around it, that it is securely fitted within the soil. You can press your hands down gently to help secure the plant within the soil.

Once you have covered your plant with soil and that it is secure within the soil, you will take your next step. On the area where you see the soil, put some sand on top of it. This doesn't have to be a mountain of sand. It should cover the soil and hide it.

Once you have done this, you have planted your Hermit Crab a plant. If you want to plant more than one plant within your Hermit Crabs crabbit, then follow the same steps as stated above. Once you have planted one plant, the rest should be easy to do.

- ***Watering Your Plants***

When you have planted all your plants, give them a light water. Your plants will probably need some watering, especially if they haven't been watered for a few hours or a day. How can you tell if they need water? You can tell they need water by doing two things. Feel the leaves of the plant and feel the base of the plant.

- ***Signs Of Dry Plants***

If the leaves of the plant are dry and the base of the plant is dry, then your plant most likely need a drink. The best way to water them is with a miniature watering can. That way, you can water them without disturbing your pet crab.

- ***Avoid Over Watering Your Plants***

What is important to note here is that you shouldn't over water your plants. Overwatering your plants is as bad as never watering them. Over watering them will make them die.

- ***Avoid Using Harmful Chemicals***

Another thing you should be careful of is what you water your plant with. Only water your plants with water. Specifically, water which is suitable for pet crabs. You never should put into plant and flower growing produce in either your water or your tank while watering the plants.

Plant and flower grower can be harmful to animals, even Hermit Crabs. They can contain poisonous chemicals in them, which could position your Hermit Crab. This will either make your Hermit Crab sick or make your Hermit Crab die. You don't want either of these things to happen, so, just the water.

The last thing that you can put in your crabbit for your Hermit Crab is some rocks. The rocks can be great for the Hermit Crab to climb over. A few tree branches and a log can also be good for this. The rocks, branches and log will help the Hermit Crab.

They will help the Hermit Crab in two ways. The first way that these things help the Hermit Crab, is that it gives them a source of entertainment. Your Hermit Crab needs something to do, so he doesn't get bored, like any other animal. Like a ball for a cat or a dog, these things can act as a source of fun for the Hermit Crab.

With the rocks, they also have another purpose. They can and will help the Hermit Crabs where you put the water for them. If they fall into the water, the rocks can help them climb out. It is the last specific thing that you need for your Hermit Crab.

Another essential item which you should install in the crabbit, which isn't for the Hermit Crabs use but is for yours, is a thermometer. The thermometer will help you to keep an eye on the temperature of the crabbit. Place this somewhere out of reach of the Hermit Crab, like on the side of the tank high up.

You should check the temperature on a regular basis. By checking it on a regular basis, you will make sure that the temperature within the crabbit is not too hot or too cold.

That is all you need for your new pet Hermit Crab. The things listed about are the essential items that you need for your Hermit Crab. A Hermit Crab does not need that many things for its survival. They can live happily and survive on just a few things. You would think that having a pet Hermit Crab is more demanding than a conventional pet.

The only thing about conventional pets, such as a pet dog or a pet cat, is that they are easier to look after. They are easier to look after because things for cats and dogs are more easily accessible. You can find things for cats and dogs in almost any store, even stores which are not pet stores.

With animals and pets such as pet Hermit Crabs, this is a bit more problematic. You are unlikely to find things for pet Hermit Crabs which are easily accessible in conventional stores. For example, it's unlikely you will find Hermit Crab food in conventional stores. This means that you will have to go to either a pet store or an online store to purchase the food.

To get buy your equipment such as sand and food and water for your Hermit Crab, it's a good idea to plan ahead and keep a journal of when you will most likely need these things. A good way to do it is to order the essentials beforehand.

In other words, you should order your food, sand and water before your run out of these things. Instead of running out of them and then ordering them. If you see these things running low, then either order the stuff online or go to the pet store and buy some new stuff for your crab.
It's probably best to get all of these things in bulk. Get your food in bulk, get your water in bulk and get your sand in bulk. If you get them in bulk, then it can save you trips and save you time. You will save yourself going to the store on a regular basis. It's also cheaper this way.

A good way to do it is to either stock up for the month or stock up on two months, in your food, water and sand. By doing this, you will save yourself the time and money. You can also tell when you are running dry on items and can make the necessary purchases beforehand - before it runs out.

Chapter 6. Your home environment

Next, you want to consider your home environment. The home environment is one of the most important aspects of a Hermit Crabs survival. The home environment you have is very important for the Hermit Crab. Your home environment must be humid at all times.

Also, your Hermit Crabs tank should be humid at all times. It should never be too hot and it should never be too cold. The environment should remain a steady humid temperature at all times. What is this humid temperature?

We are going to look at what the essential humid temperature that you should have in your home, for your Hermit Crabs tank. We shall look at this in this chapter. You should be monitoring the temperature every day when it comes to Hermit Crabs.

You will have to take into consideration a few things regarding your home environment - the things that you have to consider to ensure that your home environment is right for your Hermit Crab. You will want to make your Hermit Crab as comfortable and secure as possible.

The temperature in your Hermit Crab's crabbit should be at the right temperature at all times. What is the correct temperature for Hermit Crabs? The correct temperature for Hermit Crabs is around 72F to 75F. This is the essential temperature for your Hermit Crab.

Never let the temperature get above or below that.

Now that we've looked at the environment for your Hermit Crab tank, such as things like what temperature the tank should be. We are now going to look at what your home temperature and home environment should be like.

You will know by now that your Hermit Crab will need a humid environment. Not only should your Hermit Crabs crabbit be humid, but, your home should be humid as well.

The overall room temperature will affect your Hermit Crab. Keep that in mind when you set the room temperature. Also keep in mind when you open any windows or turn up the radiator. Keep an eye on the thermometer to make sure that you are not making the temperature too hot or too cold for your Hermit Crab.

To ensure that your home is the right temperature for your Hermit Crab, there is an easy step to ensure this. Not only should you put a thermometer in the Hermit Crabs tank, you should also put a thermometer in your living space.

This will make it easier for you to check the temperature in the room. Put the thermometer in the room. A good place is up on a wall. Don't just put the thermometer on any wall. Put it on a wall which is always going to be visible to you. In other words, put this thermometer somewhere you are always going to see it.

If you put it somewhere you are always going to see it, it will make it easier for you. You will not have to go out of your way to remember or look at the temperature from the moment. If you put the thermometer out of the way, say, in a corner of the room where you cannot see it, then, you will most likely forget.

It can be a good idea to pick a thermometer which is on a plaque or piece of wood. These thermometers are bigger and therefore more noticeable. They can also be better looking for your room.

Give Your Hermit Crab Comfort

You will want your Hermit Crab to be as comfortable as he can be. To make sure that your Hermit Crab is comfortable, always make sure your home environment is the right temperature for your crab. If the temperature is either too hot or too cold, then this can be damaging for your Hermit Crab. If the temperature is too cold for your Hermit Crab, they can suffer. They are not suited to colder environments, as they are tropical animals. If it's constantly too cold for your crab, they could die. The same is true if the temperature is the opposite.

A temperature that is too hot can be equally as damaging to the Hermit Crab as one which is too cold. If the temperature in your home is too hot, then it can have several effects on your pet crab. What are the effects of the home environment being too hot on the Hermit Crab?

The effects are as follows:

1) It can cause exhaustion in the Hermit Crab
2) It can cause dehydration in the Hermit Crab
3) It can cause the Hermit Crab to heat, or overheat

4) And, if the Hermit Crab overheats, then the crab can die

Therefore, it is extremely important that you have the right temperature in your home and within your tank. Now that you know how damaging the effects can be on your pet crab if the temperature is too hot or too cold, what is the right temperature in your home for your pet crab?

This is extremely important. To make sure that your environment is humid, keep your home environment between 72 and 75F. This will ensure that there is sufficient humidity in the air and a perfect temperature for your pet.

A good idea to make sure that your crabbit has a steady temperature and the right temperature is to put it up against a plain wall. In other words, against a wall which has no radiators or windows on it. Radiators and windows can affect the temperature. This can happen accidentally.

Protect Your Crab From The Elements

Your radiator might come on and cause the crabbit to overheat, which causes over-exhaustion and death in your crab. This is very important if you have a timer on your heater. If you have a timer on your heater and you are going to be out, it's best to place the crab away from the heater. That way you will not worry.

The same is true for windows, although windows can have the opposite effect on the home environment (causing your home to become too cold,) - it can still be as deadly as overheating.

Sometimes weather can be unpredictable, especially if you live in an area which doesn't have a steady pattern of weather. If you're out and the window is open, then it could cause a drastic drop in temperature in the room. You will want to avoid this.

A good way to avoid it is to place your Hermit Crabs crabbit away from any windows. Another way to avoid this is to close any windows if you're going out for the day. Again, you won't be worrying about it while you are out.

The temperature is just one aspect of your home environment. There are many other aspects of your home environment that you can and should

take into consideration for your new pet Hermit Crab. The next one we are going to talk about is flooring.

How To Bring Your Crab Out

You are going to want to take your Hermit Crab out of his crabbit from time to time and let him run about the place. This is a good idea if there is no danger to him - i.e. places where he can escape to, or other pets in the room can get at him. Take away anything in the room that you may think will be dangerous to your pet crab, such as your dog or cat, if you have one.

Once you have taken away anything from the room which could harm your pet crab, you will want to think about your living space, particularly your flooring.

The flooring that you have is very important for your Hermit Crab. You will need the right type of flooring, so that he can walk about with ease, without slipping. Wooden floors can be a bit problematic for Hermit Crabs, as they can find wooden floors make them slip. It's best if you have a carpet, because they can grip onto the carpet and walk on it easier.

Creating A Sand Pit For Your Crab

Another idea is to have a sand pit out for your Hermit Crab. Or, even better, a cat or dog paddling pool. Now, we're not saying to fill the dog or cat paddling pool up with water. No. Instead, you will want to fill the dog or cat paddling pool up with your sand. This can be a great way to give your Hermit Crab a larger area to walk about in and play in. That's the idea when you take your crab out.

You want to give him an area which is larger than his tank, so that he can get some exercise, walk about in and play in. A paddling pool made for dogs and cats is perfect for that. It's perfect for that for two main reasons. The first main reason is that you not only give your crab exercise, but it gives you a chance to bond and play with your crab in an open space. The second main reason is that if you put your Hermit Crab into one of these paddling pools with the sand in it, you will keep him safe.

The cat and dog paddling pools are designed to be sturdy and strong. They are made with strong plastic. And the height is tall. Which means that your crab won't escape. And therefore, he will be safe while he is out and about. Here are some guidelines when putting your crab in a paddling pool of sand:

- ***First, Prepare***

First of all, prepare the paddling pool before you bring your Hermit Crab out. You don't want your Hermit Crab wondering about, while you set your paddling pool (Hermit Crab sand pit) up.

Take your paddling pool out (if you put it away) and make it ready for the next step.

- ***Putting The Sand In***

The next step is, in putting the sand in to your paddling pool. Don't fill the paddling pool up with water, that is not the idea here. Instead, fill the paddling pool up with sand.

Leave a reasonable gap at the top of your paddling pool, so that the sand isn't on the level with the top part of your paddling pool. This will stop your Hermit Crab from escaping from the pit. If the sand is too high, then the Hermit Crab can easily climb out - which could mean he could either escape from the house or get himself hurt.

- ***Put The Equipment In***

Once you have finished putting the sand into the paddling pool, you will next want to put your Hermit Crabs equipment in the paddling pool, before you actually put the crab in itself. What is the equipment? The equipment is things such as your Hermit Crab's sea shells, rocks, twigs, logs and hidey place. That way, your Hermit Crab has something to do when he is inside the crabbit.

You can also put things such as balls in your paddling pool, or even a hamster wheel. We will speak more about that in the next chapter, when we show you how to make sure that your Hermit Crab gets plenty of exercise and how you can hold your Hermit Crab.

- ***Keep In Mind Other Pets***

This part of your home environment might not apply to all people reading this book. Taking into consideration other pets in the house will not apply to those of you who don't have other pets.

But, for those of you who do have other pets, you should be mindful of this. Particularly if you have other pets such as cats or dogs.

There are some pets that you wouldn't really need to worry about harming your pet Hermit Crab. If you had, say, a pet rabbit or hamster, then the pet hamster or rabbit is unlikely to pose a threat to your Hermit Crab.

On the contrary, if you have a pet hamster, or a pet rabbit, you should be keeping those animals away from Hermit Crabs. It's not rabbits or hamsters which could harm the Hermit Crab. It is the other way around. It is the Hermit Crab which could hurt the rabbit or hamster with his claws.

You should however take other pets into consideration if you have any, namely pet cats and pet dogs. With pet cats and pet dogs they could either get hurt from the Hermit Crabs claws, or, the Hermit Crab could hurt the cat or dog with their claws.

Both cats and dogs are known for attacking and killing animals which are smaller than them. That's not to say that the pet cat or pet dog will attack or kill your Hermit Crab, but there is a possibility that they would aim to try, or that it is instinctual behaviour.

Therefore, it is best to keep the Hermit Crab away from any cats or dogs you may have. If the Hermit Crab is attacked by a cat or dog, it will stress the Hermit Crab out. Stress inflicted upon an animal because of an attack by another animal, can and does kill.

There are several steps that you can take to protect your Hermit Crab from cats and dogs. Follow these instructions of how you can protect your Hermit Crab from cats and dogs.

- ***Have Lid A On Your Tank***

Having a lid on your tank is the best way to prevent either your cat or your dog getting at the Hermit Crab.

This is truer for cats than it is for dogs. Cats are quite notorious for getting into mischief, especially if they see another animal in a tank or a cage. The cat will try to get inside the cage or tank and jump in it. Therefore, having a lid on the tank is important if you have a cat. It will stop your cat getting into the tank, where he doesn't belong.

If you do put a lid on your Hermit Crabs tank, then make sure that the lid on the tank has holes in it. The holes in the tank are essential, as it allows the Hermit Crab to breathe. Without the holes, the Hermit Crab will suffocate and die. Therefore, it is very important that you have holes in the lid of the Hermit Crabs tank.

- ***Make Sure The Tank Is Resilient***

You should make sure that your tank is resilient. In other words, your tank should be strong and sturdy. Make sure that it is on a strong and sturdy surface. Make sure that the tank cannot fall over easily.

Both pet cats and pet dogs will knock things over. Sometimes they knock things over accidentally and sometimes they knock things over on purpose. Therefore, it becomes important to ensure your tank cannot be knocked over easily by one of your pets.

If your tank is knocked over, then it could cause several problems. The obvious problem is the mess it makes. You will have to clean everything up, all the sand and the tank could smash, because some tanks are made out of glass. There are other problems that it can cause too.

Another problem that a knocked over tank could cause (assuming that the Hermit Crab does not get hurt by the tank falling over,) is that it gives the Hermit Crab a chance to escape. This could lead them to escape out the room, even out of the house if there are spaces available to get out for him, such as a cat flap.

It also possesses another danger. If he does get out of his tank by the tank being knocked over, then there could be an accident. Someone could accidentally stand on him, because they do not know he is out. This could cause pain in the Hermit Crab or even death, but it also could cause an accident for a person.

If your Hermit Crab isn't lucky enough to escape the broken tank being knocked over, then, most likely it could kill him.

Those things are very heavy and could easily kill a Hermit Crab if they are knocked over. On a shaky or weak supporting board or desk for your tank and the whole thing could fall or collapse easily.

Taking steps to prevent these sorts of things happening is better than them happening. They are most likely not to happen, but, as we know, cats and dogs can be a bit mischievous. It's better to keep them out of the way of your Hermit Crab.

There is another group you want to keep your Hermit Crab away from, and that is small children or babies. If you have either a baby or small children in the house, then it's best to keep the Hermit Crab out of reach .

The Hermit Crab isn't really a suitable animal for small children or babies. Small children will be rough with a Hermit Crab. They don't know any better. Plus, as the Hermit Crab can get easily stressed out, the Hermit Crab might pinch a child if it is handled too roughly.

It's best to make sure kids are older, if you want to give them a Hermit Crab. When they are old enough to know how to look after the Hermit Crab and care for the Hermit Crab.

As Hermit Crabs require a lot of work, dedication, patience and care, it's probably not the most suitable pet for children. Children can get bored easily, or they don't want to do the hard jobs such as cleaning and feeding the Hermit Crab. Therefore, it's best not to buy them a Hermit Crab.

An older kid can probably have a Hermit Crab though. It's up to you though, if you have kids. A teenager would be old enough to know better, to help clean up after the pet, hold him properly and look after him properly. So, if you have an older kid and think that they are responsible enough to look after a Hermit Crab as a pet, then you should consider buying them one.

Or, if you have your own Hermit Crab and your kids are old enough, then you can let them hold the Hermit Crab too.

Taking precautions shouldn't put you off having a Hermit Crab. Prevention is better than cure. And these things are unlikely to happen with the proper care and supervision.

Hermit Crabs are amazing pets to have. There are more benefits to having a Hermit Crab, than to not having a Hermit Crab. You will get an animal you can care for and the animal in turn will care for you in their own way.

The Hermit Crab can also teach you various things. For example, as you will need to be patient with your Hermit Crab, the Hermit Crab will teach you how to be patient. This can help with all areas of your life, as it helps you to have patience in other areas of your life too.

Hermit Crabs can also help you to become more caring and compassionate in your life too, both towards other people and towards animals - as you will have to be caring and compassionate towards your Hermit Crab.

There is a lot you will learn from having a Hermit Crab. The things that you will learn from your Hermit Crab are things that you can apply to your own life, giving you a richer and more rewarding life.

The next thing that we are going to look at with regards to Hermit Crabs is in how to give your Hermit Crab exercise and how you can and should hold your Hermit Crab.

Chapter 7. Exercising And Holding Your Hermit Crab

In this chapter, we are going to look at how you can exercise your Hermit Crab and how you can hold your Hermit Crab properly.

Exercise is important for any animal and this is also true for the Hermit Crab. You will want to make sure that your Hermit Crab has plenty of exercises. Plenty of exercise will partly come down to the tank that you choose for your Hermit Crab.

You will want to make sure that it is big enough. A Hermit Crab needs a lot of space to move around in, that space gives them exercise without you having to take your Hermit Crab out for some exercise.

There are more ways to exercise your crab than just giving him a big enough space to walk and run around in. Another part of your Hermit Crabs exercise could be in letting your crab have time outside of his or her tank. This is the best way to give your Hermit Crab some exercise.

Giving your Hermit Crab the right exercise and holding him should be the most exciting and rewarding experience with your Hermit Crab. There is nothing more fun than bonding with your pet Hermit Crab through playing with him and through holding him.

Making sure that your Hermit Crab gets plenty of exercise is one of the most important ways to make sure that your Hermit Crab stays fit and healthy. Without exercise he will not have a healthy life.

It is one of the main ways of caring for your Hermit Crab. A brilliant way and a fun way to give your Hermit Crab exercise is through giving him toys. There are many toys that you can purchase for your Hermit Crab.

You will find these toys either online or in your local pet store. The Hermit Crab probably has more toys to play with than other pets, such as cats and dogs. Hermit Crabs are not limited to the toys they have.

There are two ways that you can give your Hermit Crabs toys. You can either give your Hermit Crab toys through giving your Hermit Crab simple everyday things. Or, you can give your Hermit Crab toys by buying specially made toys for Hermit Crabs, which can be found in pet stores.

Here are a few ideas for toys for your Hermit Crab:

- ***Give Them Logs***

A simple and cheap toy to give your Hermit Crab, is a log. Or, give them a few logs. Hermit Crabs love to climb over logs, it is a fun activity for the Hermit Crab to do.

There is only one rule for getting logs and putting them in your Hermit Crabs tank. You should never get logs from outside or within nature and put them in your Hermit Crabs tank. That can be harmful to the Hermit Crab, as there are insects outside which will go on the long.

What you should do instead is, buy some logs. Buying some logs will ensure that you are putting logs into your Hermit Crabs tank which have been prepared and cleaned up.

- ***Put Some Plants In***

Plants are a natural toy to the Hermit Crab. They are a way for the Hermit Crab to be entertained; it replicates their natural environment.

- ***A Hamster Wheel***

Hamster wheels are a perfect way to give your Hermit Crab a source of entertainment. Hamster wheels are a fun activity, for both you and your Hermit Crab. You can watch him while he is busy having fun on his hamster wheel.

If you want to see what a hamster wheel is like when a Hermit Crab is using it, then just do a quick Google search. There you will find pictures and articles which inform you and show you about Hermit Crabs on hamster wheels. You can even watch some videos on YouTube to show you what Hermit Crabs are like on Hamster Wheels.

- ***Give Your Hermit Crabs Balls***

Make sure they are little balls and make sure that they are not harmful to the Hermit Crab. A harmful ball will be a ball which has holes in it.

Balls can be a good way for Hermit Crabs to entertain themselves and give themselves exercise.

That's it - those are the toys that you can give to your Hermit Crab. As well as giving your Hermit Crab a fun activity, always make sure that those toys are safe for the Hermit Crab. Never give him anything that will harm him.

Now we are going to explore how to give your Hermit Crab the best exercise. And, we are also going to show you how you can hold your Hermit Crab. As they are soft and sensitive creatures, you will need to hold them in the proper way, which is with proper care.

How To Hold Your Hermit Crab

Learning how to hold your Hermit Crab is very important.

Holding your Hermit Crab is fairly straight forward and easy. It is not as intimidating as it seems. At first, it might be a bit strange holding your Hermit Crab, or even a bit of a struggle to bond with your Hermit Crab and therefore, hold your Hermit Crab. But, the more you do it, the easier it will become and the easier it will be for your Hermit Crab. Here is a guideline on how to hold your Hermit Crab:

- ***Let Him Settle First***

The first thing to do, isn't really to do with the holding process itself. Instead, it's about letting your Hermit Crab settle into his new home. Let your new Hermit Crab be familiar with his new surroundings, before you attempt to pick him up and take him out. That way, he will be more comfortable when you do come round to picking him up for the first time.

How long should you let him settle in for? You should let your Hermit Crab settle into his new home for around a week. Maybe two weeks. Then he should be settled by that point. And you can start to bond and get to know your new pet. Hermit Crabs are social animals, so, you will want to bond with your Hermit Crab and hold him as much as you can.

- ***Start Off Slowly***

Starting off slowly means trying to get your Hermit Crab to come to you first, instead of picking him up right away. You might scare him or stress him out if you just pick him up right away.

What you should do, is let him come onto your palm. Or, guide your Hermit Crab onto your palm. Do this by putting your hand, palm up, in your Hermit Crabs tank. Have patience, see if he will come to you. If he doesn't, try put your palm closer to him and gently nudge him onto your palm.

- ***Lifting Him Up***

Once you have managed to get your Hermit Crab onto your palm, bring your other palm in for support. Once you do this, lift your palms up slowly and gently. Close your palms in a bit, though not too tightly, so that your crab cannot run off the edge of your palms.

- ***Sitting Down With Him***

It's better to sit on the floor with your crab, when you have him on your palms. When your taking your crab down to the floor to sit, be gentle and slow. When you are standing up again to put your Hermit Crab back in his tank, also be gentle and slow.

- ***Avoid These Things***

When holding your Hermit Crab, there are several things that you will want to avoid. You will want to avoid being too rough with your Hermit Crab. Never bounce your Hermit Crab up and down on your palms, keep your palms relaxed at all times. Hermit Crabs can get stressed out very easily, moving your hands about will cause your crab unnecessary stress.

Holding your Hermit Crab isn't hard, it's really easy. You have to be patient, gentle and loving with your Hermit Crab. You won't be able to hold him too tightly, but, you can give him a little clap on his shell and a little cuddle if you want. All animals love being adored, the Hermit Crab is of no exception. If you treat your Hermit Crab right, you will be rewarded with an excellent companion.

- ***Exercising Your Hermit Crab***

The next thing that we want to look at is exercise. Learning how to make sure that your Hermit Crab is getting plenty of exercise, is as important as knowing how to handle your Hermit Crab. The good news is, there are various ways that you can ensure that your crab gets plenty of exercise. You can even make sure that your crab exercises when you are not with him.

To make sure that your crab gets exercise when you are not with him, there are several things that you can put in his tank. What are these things? Things such as a pile of rocks for your crab to climb on, will give him exercise. Doing the same with a log, or two logs has the same effect. If you want to give him even more exercise and let your crab be a little more adventurous, then do this:

Take pieces of food and hide them. Make sure that you hide them in places where they can eventually find the food and eat the food. This will give him something fun to do. Don't make this too difficult for him - you want to ensure that he can find the food. Doing this isn't a substitute for feeding your Hermit Crab - it is an additional game for your Hermit Crab.

- ***Giving Your Crab Toys***

There are other ways that you can help your Hermit Crab exercise. With these things, it's better to supervise your pet while letting them have access to the equipment.

There are two other ways that you can let your Hermit Crab exercise. These two things are as follows 1) Giving your Hermit Crabbit a hamster wheel, and 2) Giving your Hermit Crab some balls to play with.

With the hamster wheel and the balls, you will want to make sure that they are safe for your Hermit Crab. To make sure that these two things are safe for your Hermit Crab first, make sure that there are no holes in them.

There should be no holes in the hamster wheel and no holes in the balls. Hamster wheels and balls for pets can have holes in them and these are tricky for the crab.

Hermit Crabs only have tiny legs and this makes the hamster wheels with holes and the balls with holes dangerous to the Hermit Crab. Hermit Crabs can easily get their feet stuck in them. If they do get their feet stuck in them, then this could damage or harm their legs. This will hurt the crab.

No matter what equipment or toys you buy for your Hermit Crab, make sure that it is safe for the crab. Don't buy anything or put anything into the tank which could cause harm to your crab. Some people will say that you should a plant pot in your tank, as a hiding place for your crab.

This is actually a good idea, but, only if the plant pot is a plastic one. Don't put in a plant pot which can easily break. If you do and it breaks, you could harm your Hermit Crab.

Things like that could cut them and hurt them. So avoid putting breakable objects in your tank. A good substitute is not only plastic things, but also coconuts.

How To Set Up Your Sand Pit

A sand pit is a great way for you to bond with your Hermit Crab, give your Hermit Crab exercise and give your Hermit Crab some freedom out from his tank and into a larger area.

If you are taking your Hermit Crab out of his tank, make sure that you keep him supervised at all times. Don't leave him unsupervised and on his own.

You can help your Hermit Crab exercise by setting up a sand pit in your home. You can either make this a permanent set up, or, you can fold it up and put it away when you are not using it. We've touched on this before, but let's take a more in-depth of how you can do this.

Buy Your Perfect Sand Pit

There are two ways that you can do this. You can either buy a sand pit which is made for children. Or, you can buy a paddling pool which is made for cats and dogs. The paddling pools which are made for cats and dogs are bigger than children's sand pits, and therefore it will give your Hermit Crab more space to move about in when you take your crab out.

Two Things Never To Do

Whatever one you choose to go with, there are two things that you should never do. The first thing that you should never do is fill your pool or your pit up with water. This is not about giving them water to go into. This is about giving them a larger area to play in. An area with sand.

The second thing that you should never do is fill the sand pit or the pool up with children's sand, play sand or any other sand which is not made for Hermit Crabs. Like the sand in your Hermit Crabs tank, this sand that you put in should be sand which is for suitable for the Hermit Crab.

Put The Toys And Equipment In

Before you take out your Hermit Crab and put him in the pool or pit, prepare the area. Don't take your Hermit Crab out before hand and have him wandering about. You might accidental stand on him while you're busy making up his area. It's better that he is safe while you are doing this.

You will want to prepare this area in much the same way that you prepared your Hermit Crabs tank. First, you will have to put in the sand. Make sure that the sand doesn't fill the pool or pit, as we have advised before. Leave a gap at the top, so that your crab cannot get out and escape.

Once you have done this, put things into the pool or pit that the crab can play with. These things include their rocks, their sea shells and their logs, all of these things will be in the tank. Just take them out and put them in the sand. You can also put in the hamster wheel or the balls.

Bonding And Playing

This is where you get to bond and play with your Hermit Crab. Once you have successfully set up the area, take your Hermit Crab out of his tank gently and slowly put him down in the fresh sand. From here on in, you can watch your Hermit Crab run around or play.

You can even play with the Hermit Crab too. The balls are an excellent way to play with your Hermit Crab; you can roll the balls and watch your crab play with them. A fun and entertaining way of bonding with your crab and letting your crab bond with you.

Feeding And Watering

If you are taking your crab out for a while, a few hours, then give your crab some food and water after a while. The activities will probably make him thirsty and hungry.

Put the bowls which are in his tank, inside this area. He should have access to some fresh water, some salt water and some food. He will need this energy after a while, the energy from the food and water.

Playtime Over

Lastly, when play time is over make sure that you put your Hermit Crab back in his tank. Don't let him run about unsupervised on his own, especially if you have other pets.

Putting him back in his tank means that he is safe and secure. Gently put him back in his tank. If you see him starting to get tired beforehand, or see him starting to fall asleep, then you should put him back in his tank. He's probably exhausted himself.

Cleaning Up

Once you have put your crab back into his home, it's time to clean up. Put the crabs food and water back inside the tank. Also put in his rocks, sea shells and logs. Depending on how much room the pit or pool takes up, you can either fold it up and put it away, or you can just leave it there for the next time.

Caring and bonding with your pet crab is such an easy and enjoyable activity. An activity which will usually have to be done at night. In the next chapter, we are going to look at the nocturnal nature of the Hermit Crab.

Chapter 8. The Hermit Crab's Nocturnal Nature

The Hermit Crab is a nocturnal animal. Therefore, you will mostly see your Hermit Crab awake at night. Cats are also nocturnal animals, but it doesn't affect the fact that people keep cats successfully as pets. And neither will it affect the fact of keeping a Hermit Crab as a nocturnal pet. Therefore, let's take a look at the Hermit Crab as a nocturnal pet.

You will probably have to do all of your activity with and for your Hermit Crab at night. This is because of the Hermit Crabs nocturnal nature. Your Hermit Crab won't wake up at the same time every night, but, they will probably wake up at a similar time each night. Usually, Hermit Crabs start waking up the minute the sun goes down and darkness falls.

Hermit Crabs like being in the dark. That is why they are nocturnal animals. Plus, in the wild when they are active during the night as they face fewer predators. For example, they are less likely to be hunted on land by species of birds or caught in fishing nets at night, compared with during the day. This is partly why they have evolved to be nocturnal animals; to avoid nearby predators.

The Behaviour Of The Hermit Crab

Another reason is they just love the darkness. This is why the Hermit Crab will bury itself underneath the sand. They bury themselves underneath the sand because it is darker down there, than on the surface of the sand. Plus, in the wild, they can hide underneath the sand from predators. Being underneath the sand can be a place of security for the Hermit Crab.

Another reason the Hermit Crab digs underneath the sand is because either they are shedding their skin, or, they are about to shed their skin. This is called moulting their skin. If you see your Hermit Crab moulting their skin, then he is going to need a bit of special care and attention at this time. Young crabs in particular like to dig underneath the sand when they are moulting.

The moulting phase of a Hermit Crabs life can be a bit confusing for them - which is part of the reason the younger ones bury underneath the sand. They haven't shed their skin before, so this is a new experience for them. It can also be a very stressful event for Hermit Crabs, even the older ones.

There is conflicting advice out there about whether or not you should pick up your Hermit Crab when he is moulting his skin. Some of the advice you will come across will say that you should pick him up. While other people will tell you that you shouldn't pick him up. So, what do you do?

It's probably best that you don't pick up your Hermit Crab when he is moulting. But, at the same time, keep a close eye on him. Hermit Crabs are even more vulnerable when they are shedding their skin through the moulting phase - they are more sensitive and are stressed during this period. For these reasons, it's better not to pick him up. He'll probably just stress more.

So, how do you know if your Hermit Crab is in the moulting phase?

There are several ways that you can tell if your crab is in the moulting phase. Here are some signs that your crab is shedding his skin.

- ***Bigger Appetite***

Your Hermit Crab will start to eat more during this phase. That's one of the signs that you can tell he is in the phase of shedding his skin.

- ***He Turns Pink***

If you see that your crab is turning a different colour, usually pink, then your Hermit Crab is shedding his skin, most likely.

- ***He Goes Under The Sand***

Now, this isn't an automatic sign that your Hermit Crab is shedding his skin. Just because he is burying underneath the sand, doesn't necessarily mean that he is in the phase of shedding his skin. However, it can be a sign that he is either ready to shed his skin, or is in the process of shedding his skin.

- ***He Actually Sheds His Skin***

This one is obvious. If you see your Hermit Crab shedding off his skin, then that is obviously what he is doing. Don't pick it off - that could hurt him. Instead, let the skin come off naturally.

It's most likely that your Hermit Crab will shed his skin throughout the night without you being there. That's okay. Your Hermit Crab will also do all of his other activities throughout the night. This includes, eating, drinking, playing and hiding.

When you are taking your crab out of his tank to play with, or if you are cleaning your Hermit Crabs tank, don't do it throughout the day. Your Hermit Crab will be sleeping. Do these things at night when you see that your Hermit Crab has woken up. If you wake your crab up during the day, he may pinch you with his pincers. This isn't his fault - he probably got a fright by being disturbed in his sleep. If you do ever find your crab pinching you, then rinse your finger under cold water.

Never rinse the Hermit Crab under cold water though. You might panic if he pinches you, don't do that. If you panic he may grip on tighter, because he feels even more stress. Being calm will make the crab release his grip quicker. He might not even grip though, he may just pinch you.

Watching when your crab wakes up can help avoid this - it will give you an idea of when you can see your pet, when you can play with him and when he is active.

Chapter 9. Getting The Most out Of Your New Pet

Now that you know what a Hermit Crab is, you know how to look after your new Hermit Crab and what he or she needs, we are now going to look at how you can get the most out of your new found pet in this last chapter of this book. There are several ways to get the most out of your pet crab.

So, how can you get the most out of your new Hermit Crab? Let us take a look.

There are two main ways that you can get the most out of your new pet. The first way to get the most out of your new pet is to look after your Hermit Crab well. The second way to get the most out of your new pet is to enjoy having your pet crab. Let us take these two points further.

One of the best ways to get the most out of your new pet is to look after him well. If you look after your pet well, then he will have a happy life. Not only that, but you can increase his chances of surviving longer if you look after him well. When Hermit Crabs have a good diet, the right water (both fresh water and salt water), a comfortable place to live which is cleaned out on a regular basis and some love, care and affection from you, and your pet crab will live a longer life.

This is the same for any pet. If you look after them well and properly, then you will have a pet which has a long life, a healthy life and one which is a happy life for them. However, if you neglect your pet, then you can cause unhappiness, stress, illness and even death in your pet. Therefore, properly caring for your pet is the first and most important way to get the most out of your pet.

The second way to get the best out of your new pet is, to enjoy the experience. Enjoying having your pet is a rewarding and fulfilling way to get the most out of your Hermit Crab.

Sometimes life can move past quickly, or we just don't enjoy living in the moment, because of the stresses of life, which in turn causes us not to appreciate the moments that we are in. When we are not in those moments and those moments are gone, we then regret not enjoying or appreciate those moments that we were in. Think about if you've lost a pet before - at times you can wish for those moments to come back, so that you can spend more time with your pet.

If you think about it that way, then you can maximize your time with your pet and not take that time for granted when spending that time with your pet. Enjoy the time you have with your pet. Not only will you enjoy your time in the moment, you will also enjoy your time in the future when you reflect back.

Things To Avoid With Your Crab

Getting the most out of your new pet also means learning about the things which you should avoid with your new Hermit Crab.

Let us take a look at the things that you should avoid giving your Hermit Crabs.

- ***The Food You Should Avoid Giving Your Crab***

As you have learned by now, Hermit Crabs will eat almost anything that you give them. Though, this is not always a good thing. There are certainly foods that you should avoid giving to your Hermit Crab.

There are several foods which are harmful for the Hermit Crabs. If the Hermit Crab eats these foods, they it will poison him. So, it's best avoided. These are the food that you should avoid giving to your Hermit Crab, most of them are not things you would think about giving him anyway, as most of them are plants.

The foods and plants to avoid giving to the Hermit Crab are; buttercups, carnations, bindweed, alder bark, cinnamon, eucalyptus, garlic, Holly, mistletoe, peppermint, onion, daisies, lavender, lemon grass, ivy, rosemary and yew.

These are just some of the things that you should avoid giving to your Hermit Crab. That avoids giving them to your Hermit Crab to eat or just putting them in their tank, as they will poison your Hermit Crab and either make him ill or kill him.

While these are a list of the foods and plants that you should avoid giving to your Hermit Crab for any reason, there are other ones that you can give to your Hermit Crab. Let us take a look at the foods and plants that you can give to your Hermit Crab.

These are just some of the foods and plants that you can give to your Hermit Crab. They are: avocados, blackberries, bananas, carrots, blackberries, apples, almonds, clovers, coconuts, cod liver oil, fish, cucumber, cranberries, cooked eggs, corn, corn flowers, grapes, jasmine flowers, passion fruit, peaches, pears, oysters, oranges, mushrooms, raspberry, raisins, strawberries and potatoes.

All of these things can be eaten by Hermit Crabs. You can either cook these foods or give them to your Hermit Crab raw. Of course it depends on what kind of food it is you're giving to your Hermit Crab. You can give him a variety of tasty foods.

- ***Never Put Granite Or Mental Inside Of The Tank***

You should never have granite or metal inside of your Hermit Crabs tank. Granite and metal are poisonous to Hermit Crabs.

Some owners will put granite at the bottom of the Hermit Crabs tank. You should never do this, never put granite at the bottom of your Hermit Crabs tank. Not only is it poisonous to Hermit Crabs, it is also highly unsuitable to put in their tank.

You should always be putting sand in the Hermit Crabs tank. The sand is what they should have. And, not just any sand either. You should be putting in the proper sand, which we spoke about earlier in this book. Never put sand like playing sand in your Hermit Crabs tank - again, unsuitable for the Hermit Crab.

Another thing that you should be avoiding is metal. Avoid putting metal in your Hermit Crabs tank at all costs. You are probably not just going to put a piece of metal in the tank, you'd probably do it accidentally.

You might accidentally put metal bowls or metal toys in the Hermit Crabs tank and this should also be avoided at all costs. Metal is highly poisonous to Hermit Crabs and it will kill them.

Another common thing that happens with new or inexperienced owners of Hermit Crabs is, people putting Hermit Crabs in metal cages. These cages are like hamster cages. This should be avoided too, as the metal on the cages will also poison Hermit Crabs.

- ***Never Give Your Crab Meat***

The last thing on the list that you should avoid giving your Hermit Crab is, any sort of meat. Giving your Hermit Crab fish is okay. Hermit Crabs can eat fish and they do eat fish in the wild.

However, Hermit Crabs do not eat meat in the wild, especially the raw meat of farm animals such as cows, chickens and pigs. Therefore, you should never give your Hermit Crab things such as raw meat or meat itself.

Giving either raw meat or cooked meat to a Hermit Crab could give them food poison or make them unwell. It's best to avoid it at all costs. They wouldn't particularly like raw meat or cooked meat anyway, as they are not accustomed to it. They are not used to these kinds of foods and that is why it can make them unwell.

Now you know the things to avoid giving your Hermit Crab. Avoiding giving things to your Hermit Crab is part of caring and looking after your Hermit Crab. You should know and learn about the things that you should avoid giving to your Hermit Crab.

This is part of looking after them. Part of looking after them is avoiding things which are bad for them, as well as giving them the things which are good for them. That is the mark of a responsible owner, which of course you will be.

Before we conclude with this final chapter, we are going to look at two other things. The first thing that we are going to look at is the reproduction of Hermit Crabs. The second thing that we are going to look at is the personality of Hermit Crabs.

We will take these two points step-by-step:

Like with any other animal, both in the wild, and in captivity, the reproduction of Hermit Crabs is the most important part of their survival. Without Hermit Crabs reproducing, they would become extinct.

This is especially important in today's climate, as several species of Hermit Crab are endangered to extinction. Without reproducing, these Hermit Crabs will become extinct in the wild. That's bad news for the species of Hermit Crab and bad news for the entire ecosystem.

Ecosystems depend upon all animals and plants playing their part to make the ecosystem survive and thrive. If parts of the ecosystem disappear from the habitat, in other words become extinct, then the whole ecosystem is vulnerable to collapsing.

Although it doesn't seem like one species of animal would have such a detrimental impact to an entire system, it can, and it has, happened before. The thing is that the entire ecosystem is interconnected - if one part of the ecosystem falls down (disappears.), then it is like a domino effect where all other parts of the ecosystem suffer.

Therefore, single species such as Hermit Crabs can and do make an impact in the wild. Therefore, it is important for them to reproduce to ensure the survival of the species in the future.

You can even help the species survive by helping to breed them yourself, like we have shown you earlier in the book.

The reproduction of Hermit Crabs is a particularly fascinating spectacle to watch. The female Hermit Crabs will literally have thousands of eggs in each reproduction cycle. They will carry these into the water to help them to reproduce.

The Hermit Crab does not reproduce on land. It is not a suitable environment for them to reproduce and they are not comfortable reproducing on land, due to them being easily exposed to predators such as birds.

As they would be out in the open, with little to no cover, it is dangerous for the Hermit Crab to reproduce in the open air. Therefore, they take this to the sea, where they can have privacy and hide from predators who would eat them otherwise.

This whole reproduction cycle and activity will happen in the sea for wild Hermit Crabs. If they are on land, the female Hermit Crabs will go into the sea to find a mate to reproduce. Then, the female Hermit Crab will give birth in the ocean.

The female Hermit Crab will hide the eggs somewhere on the sea floor bed. Eventually, over time, these eggs will become baby Hermit Crabs.

Gestation doesn't last long for female Hermit Crabs. They will give birth around a month after the initial pregnancy began and they will do this by laying the eggs on the sea floor.

Once the female Hermit Crab has layer the eggs on the ocean floor, she will then leave them alone. She will leave them alone until it is time for the Hermit Crab eggs to hatch. Then the mother will come back to the hatching eggs.

The Personality Of The Hermit Crab

The way that the female Hermit Crab behaves during reproduction is part of the personality of the Hermit Crab - but, there is a lot more to their personality than just this.

The Hermit Crabs are fascinating animals with a lot of personality. It is in their personality which makes this little species charming and adorable. They might be small, but Hermit Crabs have a lot of spirit.

Like with all animals, no two Hermit Crabs are exactly the same. And therefore, no two Hermit Crabs have the exact same personality. They are all unique and therefore, they are all different in personality.

So, what are the main personality traits of the Hermit Crab? Let's take a look at the main personality traits of the Hermit Crab.

Part of the Hermit Crabs personality is to be sociable and fun loving animals. They like to be at the centre of the action, surrounded by other Hermit Crabs. And, they also like to have fun, which is why it's a great idea to give these pets some toys.

Another part of their personality is in being very mischievous. Hermit Crabs are very mischievous in behaviour. They seem to like to get into a bit of trouble, especially when they are kept as a pet.

As pets in tanks, the Hermit Crab will act mischievously by tossing his food and water dishes over. It is a common behaviour in Hermit Crabs as pets. You will never be bored of a Hermit Crab.

Conclusion and Summary

Hermit Crabs are an amazing pet and you will have a delightful new pet, one which is full of character and spirit. We hope that you have learned a lot from this book. The first thing that you started to learn in this book was about Hermit Crabs in the wild.

In the second half of the book you learned about Hermit Crabs as pets and how to look after them as pets. Because you have learned about both Hermit Crabs as pets and Hermit Crabs in the wild, you have an excellent foundation for starting on your journey.

By now, you have learned everything that there is to know about Hermit Crabs. You've learned about Hermit Crabs both in the wild and as a pet, how to look after them, and how to care for them.

Hermit Crabs are wonderful animals and they are wonderful pets to have too. It's not unusual to come across someone with a pet cat or dog, but it is a bit unusual to come across a person with a Hermit Crab as a pet. The Hermit Crab is a very cool pet to have!

Your exotic new pet will impress everyone you know.

As there are several species of Hermit Crab, 1000 species in the wild, you are going to have to choose the right Hermit Crab for yourself. There are two types of Hermit Crab you will probably choose from.

These are the two types of Hermit Crab that are most commonly sold as pets. They Are the Ecuadorian Hermit Crab and the Caribbean Hermit Crab. Both the Ecuadorian Hermit Crab and the Caribbean Hermit Crab are different species of Hermit Crab.

The Ecuadorian Hermit Crab is a bit smaller than the Caribbean Hermit Crab, and it is also less exotic looking. The Caribbean Hermit Crab is the prettier of the two. It comes in a gorgeous pink and white colour, the shell is white and the body is pink.

Both of these species of Hermit Crab are delightful in their own right.

No matter what species of Hermit Crab you choose to buy, you can apply the knowledge that you have found in this book towards keeping them as a pet - the knowledge about what a Hermit Crab is and the knowledge about how to keep and look after a Hermit Crab as a pet. This book is a great guide to Hermit Crabs. You should read it a few times to make yourself as familiar about the Hermit Crab as possible.

The more you learn about the Hermit Crab, the more your will know about the Hermit Crab. The first thing that you have learned in this book is about Hermit Crabs in the wild.

Hermit Crabs can be found all over the world, usually in exotic places. Though, they are not only found in exotic places. They can also be found in places which don't have tropical weather; such as the United Kingdom and other parts of Europe.

You won't find Hermit Crabs in every country and in every habitat. Though, they are a versatile bunch who can live in a wide variety of habitats. This in itself is one of the reasons that Hermit Crabs are so impressive. It shows that they are a strong and resilient animal.

This is uncommon for most species of animals. Most animal species are only found in one or two continents and in one or two types of habitat and climate. This is not true in the case of the Hermit Crab.

Most animals are also land animals or marine animals; again, this is not true for the Hermit Crab. These two points show that the Hermit Crab is a resilient animal.

An animal which can stand various ecosystems.

The downside of this is that Hermit Crabs are exposed to more predators in the wild.

They have more animals which will attack them, kill them or eat them. Even other Hermit Crabs will attack, kill or eat Hermit Crabs. This is why Hermit Crabs have evolved to hide under shells.

Hiding under shells protects them from predators. Predators such as fish in the ocean, or birds on land.

While in captivity, Hermit Crabs don't have these threats. This can make the life of a Hermit Crab easier and less stressful as a pet.

They can be very adorable pets, which don't require a lot of work. Looking after a pet Hermit Crab is a treasure. They are straight forward animals to look after.

To have a pet Hermit Crab, you will first have to buy your equipment for your new pet.

The things that you will have to buy for your Hermit Crab is (1) A tank, which is also known as a crabbit, (2) Sand and substrate, (3) A thermometer, (4) Toys, rocks, logs, twigs and a hiding place for your crab, and (5) A sand pit for when you want to take your crab out to play.

These are the basic things you need for your pet crab. It isn't a lot. And it's not really that much more than say, if you were buying for a hamster or rabbit.

All of these things can either be purchased online, on Amazon, or at your local pet store. They will create a happy and fulfilling life for your new pet Hermit Crab.

An essential part of caring for your Hermit Crab is giving them the right diet. An all-round balanced diet for your Hermit Crab is of the utmost importance. You should be feeding your crab specific food.

You will want to make sure that your Hermit Crab has fresh food on a daily basis. Give him some specialized Hermit Crab food on a daily basis. Never leave food in the tank too long. If food is left for days, it can begin to go off and go mould.

This will make your Hermit Crab unwell, if he is either eating or exposed to rotten food. There is also another thing that leaving old food around can cause, and that is mites. Mites will thrive off of rotting food, so you want to avoid it at all costs.

Along with having a dish full of fresh food every day, you will also want to give your Hermit Crab two other dishes in his tank.

These two dishes are water dishes. There should be one water dish for your fresh water and another water dish for your salt water.

There are two pieces of advice here. The first piece of advice is to never ever give your Hermit Crab tap water. Because tap water has chemicals in it and because tap water can have traces of metal in it, the tap water can and will kill the Hermit Crab.

You should stick to giving your Hermit Crab water made for the Hermit Crab. And that water is fresh water and salt water.

The second piece of advice that you should take on board is to never give your Hermit Crab table salt. Table salt can and will have the same effect as tap water towards the Hermit Crab. Table salt is very damaging for them. Instead, make sure that your salt water is also specifically made for your Hermit Crab (containing sea salt).

We then looked at where you should get started on your journey to having a pet Hermit Crab. Most of you are probably unfamiliar with the Hermit Crab, because they are an exotic and rare pet. Therefore, we dedicated a chapter for you in how you can get started on your journey to buying and keeping a pet Hermit Crab.

Buying and keeping a pet Hermit Crab is easy. You can either buy all of the items at one of the big pet stores, or, you can buy it all online. It doesn't really matter where you buy the Hermit Crab's necessities, as long as it is good quality and suitable for the species, then it is good. But, you might be wondering where to buy your Hermit Crab? Let us take a look.

You can buy Hermit Crabs in pet stores. You will be able to get advice on Hermit Crabs and the store assistant will show you what equipment to get, they can advise you.

If you are looking for some places to buy your Hermit Crab's equipment from online, then below we are going to give you a good list of links (please be aware that all of these websites were active at the time of writing this book – and that may not be the case now, which is, of course, out of our control):

The Crabby Cravings: www.crabbycravings.co.uk

Pet Smart: www.petsmart.com

That Pet Place: www.thatpetplace.com

The Sea Shell Patch: www.seashellshop.com

Pet Shop Direct: www.petshopdirect.com.au

Of course, you can also use Amazon as well, as they have a good selection of Hermit Crab essentials. All of these online shops have a home delivery option. It will help save you the journey of going out to the pet store. Instead, you can get the items delivered.

This can be particularly helpful with heavier stuff, such as sand. Sand can be heavy to carry, especially the bigger sacks - so you can always order the sand online and make it easier for yourself.

Shopping for your pet Hermit Crab is fun. You can buy things which will help him to have fun and entertain him.

The chapter early on in the book about 'Where To Get Started,' is designed not only to help you as an easy step-by-step guide to looking after and caring for your pet Hermit Crab. It is also designed for you to print out. By printing out this chapter, you can follow along the guidelines easily and effortlessly.

With this guide you are going to learn how you can set up your Hermit Crab and what you should put in your crabbit. This part is very important and something that you should do, *before*, you put their Hermit Crab in his new crabbit.

A Hermit Crabs crabbit should consist of a few items. There is not that many items that will need to go in the crabbit. These items are the essential items - items which your Hermit Crab will definitely need for its survival.

You should be putting these essential items in your pet Hermit Crabs crabbit:

- Sand
- Substrate
- Hermit Crab Food
- Fresh water for the crab
- Salt water for the crab
- Some plants for your crab
- A hiding place for your crab
- And, some toys for your crab

That's it. These are the essential items you need for your pet crab. You can find all of these essential items in chapter 5 of the book.

Anything else that is mentioned in the book is a bonus for your pet Hermit Crab. However, you should try and make your Hermit Crab's life as fun and fulfilling as possible.

In chapter six we looked at the home environment and your home environment's relation to the Hermit Crab. The home environment is a very important aspect for your Hermit Crab. It's so important, that the environment of your home is as important as giving your Hermit Crab food and water.

The home environment is something that you should always be keeping an eye on. You can do this by installing a thermometer in your home, as that will help you to monitor the temperature easily. Have two thermometers. Have a thermometer in your Hermit Crab's tank and have a thermometer in your room, preferably on your wall where you can see it.

The temperature in your home should always be a humid temperature. It should never be too hot or too cold. If the temperature is too hot, it will kill the Hermit Crab. If the temperature is too cold, it will also kill the Hermit Crab.

The right temperature for the Hermit Crab is around 72F or 75F - that is a good humid temperature for the Hermit Crab to live and thrive on. To make sure that this temperature is kept at all times, make sure that you keep your Hermit Crab's tank away from radiators and windows.

In chapter seven we looked at exercising and holding your pet Hermit Crab. You will want to make sure that your Hermit Crab gets a lot of exercise. He will need a lot of exercise to keep fit and healthy. There are several ways to make sure that he gets a lot of exercise.

Two good ways of making sure that your Hermit Crab gets plenty of exercise is, 1) give your Hermit Crab toys to play with, and 2) bring your Hermit Crab out of his crabbit regularly.

If you do these two things, not only will you be giving your Hermit Crab plenty of exercise, you will also be giving yourself a rewarding experience.

You will be having a lot of fun with your Hermit Crab, but you will also be bonding with him.

Another way to bond with your Hermit Crab is to hold him. And to hold him on a regular basis. Your Hermit Crab needs to be held on a regular basis so he can become familiar with you and comfortable with you. We should you how you can hold your Hermit Crab.

Holding your Hermit Crab is simple, though it may require a little patience. You should always be caring and patient when you are holding your pet Hermit Crab. Never be rough or inconsiderate.

While in chapter eight, we looked at the nocturnal nature of Hermit Crabs. The Hermit Crab is a nocturnal animal, even in the wild they are nocturnal animals, though, sometimes they can be spotted throughout the say. As a pet though, you are most likely to see your Hermit Crab at night time.

Your pet Hermit Crab will wake up around night fall. Perhaps a bit later than that, sometimes Hermit Crabs can wake up later in the evening. Which can be challenging for a pet owner.

The fact that your Hermit Crab wakes up at night is one of the few challenges that you will face owning a Hermit Crab. It is a challenge because you will have to do everything with him at night time.

All of your activities and bonding will have to be done at night. You will have to feed and water him at night. You will have to play with him at night. And, you will have to clean out his tank at night.

You will therefore probably want to do things such as clean out his tank at the weekend. This is because you have more free time at the weekend, and can stay up later. Which gives you plenty of time to clean out the tank and put fresh sand, food and water in it.

Night-time is also the time you should be bonding with your Hermit Crab, due to your Hermit Crab's nocturnal nature.

You should never wake your Hermit Crab up during the day to play with him, nor for any other reason. Leave him alone to sleep throughout the day - a good sleep is essential for their health and well-being. Disrupted sleep will take a toll on their health and make them ill. So, leave him alone during the day.

In the last chapter, chapter nine, we looked at how to get the best out of your Hermit Crab. And, that is what we are going to finish this book with – how to get the best out of your Hermit Crab.

Getting the best out of your Hermit Crab is the most rewarding aspect of having a pet Hermit Crab. If you get the best out of your Hermit Crab, then you will make your Hermit Crab happy and you will make yourself happy. Both of you are winners, which makes a rich experience for the both of you. To get the most out of your Hermit Crab as a pet, look after him well, bond with him regularly, and you should learn as much as you can about the species of Hermit Crabs.

We hope that you have enjoyed this book and took some good and useful tips away from it. Have fun with your new pet. Good luck in finding a great Hermit Crab friend and thank you for purchasing this book.

Printed in Great Britain
by Amazon

24399643R00056